# Psychogeography

## Other books by Will Self

### Fiction

The Quantity Theory of Insanity

Cock & Bull

My Idea of Fun

Grey Area

The Sweet Smell of Psychosis

Tough, Tough Toys for Tough, Tough Boys

Great Apes

Dorian

How the Dead Live

Dr Mukti and Other Tales of Woe

The Book of Dave

### Non-fiction

Junk Mail

Sore Sites

Perfidious Man

Feeding Frenzy


## Other books by Ralph Steadman

### Written and Illustrated

Sigmund Freud

I Leonardo

The Big I Am

The Scar-Strangled Banner

Doodaaa (novel)

The Joke's Over: Memories of Hunter S. Thompson (memoir)

### Illustrated

Fear and Loathing in Las Vegas

Alice

Animal Farm

The Devil's Dictionary

# Psychogeography

Disentangling the Modern Conundrum of Psyche and Place

Words by Will Self

Pictures by Ralph Steadman

BLOOMSBURY

Text copyright © by Will Self 2003, 2004, 2005, 2006, 2007
Illustrations copyright © by Ralph Steadman 2003, 2004, 2005, 2006, 2007

Author, artist, and publisher gratefully acknowledge that with the exception of the introduction and its
images, all the other words and pictures in this book were first published in the *Independent* newspaper in
their "Psychogeography" column between 2003 and 2007.

Published by Bloomsbury USA, New York
Distributed to the trade by Holtzbrinck Publishers

All papers used by Bloomsbury USA are natural, recyclable products made from wood grown in
well-managed forests. The manufacturing processes conform to the environmental regulations
of the country of origin.

LIBRARY OF CONGRESS CATALOGING-IN-PUBLICATION DATA HAS BEEN APPLIED FOR.

ISBN-10 1-59691-466-1
ISBN-13 978-1-59691-466-7

First U.S. Edition 2007

10 9 8 7 6 5 4 3 2 1

Text design and typesetting by Polly Napper
Printed in Singapore by Tien Wah Press

For Kurt Vonnegut, Jr.,
writer, wit and sage
(1916–2007)

Drawn on a paper tablecloth at Lasagna Ristorante,
corner of 2nd Avenue and 50th, New York, October 2006

# Contents

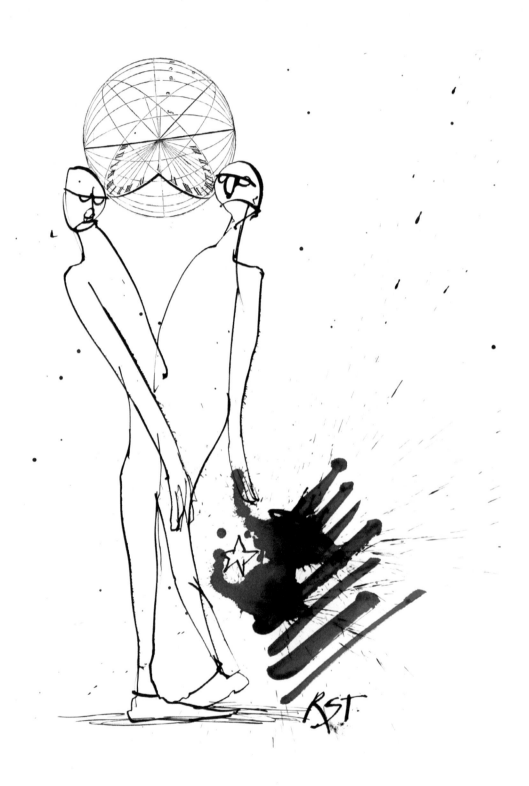

# Walking to New York

'Honor escapes he who runs after it'
Jewish proverb, from my great-grandfather's notebook

## Prologue

I resolved to walk to New York; in the interests of writing about the experience, certainly, yet also with objectives at once more pedestrian and more ambitious.

This was, perhaps, to be the defining journey so far as my particular brand of psychogeography is concerned. Although we psychogeographers are all disciples of Guy Debord and those rollicking Situationists who tottered, soused, across the stage set of 1960s Paris, thereby hoping to tear down the scenery of the Society of the Spectacle with their devilish *dérive*, there are still profound differences between us. While we all want to unpick this conundrum, the manner in which the contemporary world warps the relationship between psyche and place, the ways in which we go about the task, are various.

Some see psychogeography as concerned with the personality of place itself. Thus, in his novels and biographies, Peter Ackroyd practises a 'phrenology' of London. He feels up the bumps of the city and so defines its character and proclivities. To read Ackroyd is to become aware that while the physical and political structure of London may have mutated down the ages, as torrents of men and women coursed through its streets, yet their individuality is as nothing, set beside the city's own enduring personification.

Others, such as my friend Nick Papadimitriou, pursue what he prefers to term 'deep topography': minutely detailed, multi-level examinations of select locales that impact upon the writer's own microscopic inner-eye. He manufactures slides,

11

in which are pinioned ecology, history, poetry and sociology. Nick points out that most of the psychogeographic fraternity (and, dispiritingly, we are a fraternity: middle-aged men in Gore-Tex, armed with notebooks and cameras, stamping our boots on suburban station platforms, politely requesting the operators of tea kiosks in mossy parks to fill our thermoses, querying the destinations of rural buses. Our prostates swell as we crunch over broken glass, behind the defunct brewery on the outskirts of town) are really only local historians with an attitude problem. Indeed, real, professional local historians view us as insufferably bogus and travelling – if anywhere at all – right up ourselves.

On the night before I set off to walk to New York, my wife looked quizzically at me, as one might regard someone who, whether through disorganisation or ineptitude, had ended up making a journey both senseless and tedious, and, putting her head charmingly on one side, said: 'Remind me again, why is it that you're going to New York?'

Doubtless there was an element of affectionate ribbing in this: she knows that I know that she knows that I know, that while she views my psychogeographic peregrinations as marching along the poorly marked, crinkle-cut frontier between boredom and pretension, she nonetheless not only encourages, but even enjoins them, because of their beneficial impact on my mental health, and, by extension, that of our family.

A digression: do I believe that men are corralled in this field due to certain natural and/or nurtured characteristics, that lead us to believe we have – or actually do inculcate us with – superior visual-spatial skills to women, and an inordinate fondness for all aspects of orientation, its pursuit, minutiae and – worst of all – accessories? Absolutely. And so, while not altogether abandoning the fantasy of encountering a psychogeographic muse who will make these jaunts still more pleasurable, poignant and emotionally revelatory than they already are, in my continent heart I understand that I am fated to wander alone, or at best with one other, occasional . . . male companion.

I will answer my wife's question for you – but not yet. Mine are not writerly journeys in the accepted sense: Rousseau philosophising *à pied*, Goethe rattling into Switzerland in a coach, Cobbett on his clopping gee-gee, assorted Borrows and Stevensons plodding with their donkeys, Greene rocking on a train, Thesiger with a camel up his arse. Even in the modern era there remain writers firmly convinced that there are still discoverable terrains – human, physical, cultural – and ways of traversing them, so as to be able to convey their 'novelty' in words. I am not of their number.

I find it uncanny to be in a world in which, as I write this very sentence, I will travel thirty or forty miles through the upper atmosphere, while – in search of the *mot juste* – glancing either over the shoulder of the kidult watching *The Ant Bully* or at the photographic scenes of Oxford colleges – in all their bluey verdancy – that adorn the bulkheads of this Boeing 757 aircraft, on its flight from JFK to Heathrow.

I can only speak for myself: a mammoth depression tramples me, and my mind reaches vanishing point as it negligently orbits the planet; to think, at all, of taking a package tour to visit the Ituri pygmies of the Congolese rainforest, or fostering a globalised economy that will, in the fullness of its exaltation, make it possible for them to visit me.

No. I resolved to walk to New York because I wanted to explore. Here was a true Empty Quarter, and, as with other long walks I have taken out of my native city, I had the strong hunch that this would be the first time in the post-industrial era that anyone had ventured across it. True, I had walked from central London to Heathrow before, and I had heard of one adventurer who had walked from JFK to Manhattan, but I was certain I would be the first person to go the whole way, with only the mute, incurious interlude of a club class seat to interfere with the steady, two-mile-an-hour, metronomic rhythm of my legs, parting and marrying, parting and marrying.

This is one part of the answer to my wife's question; the second is to observe that I had *reasons* to go to New York: relatives to see, a writers' residency to launch, an interview in connection with the US publication of one of my novels. Whatever my wife thought (or thought I didn't think).

This was what distinguishes my psychogeography from that of the others. This was to be no randomised transit, intended to outfox prescribed folkways. (You read of such things, on the web, natch: proceeding across Toronto by throwing a dice, journeying to unlovely parts of Florence with carefully contrived non-deliberation.) And nor was it to be like the treks undertaken by Iain Sinclair, that Celtic Englishman whose circumnavigation of the M25 (London's orbital motorway), or travail along the A13 to Southend, were dogged, shamanic attempts to storm these concrete bastions – with their bark-chip, shrubbery-planted revetments – laying siege with the trebuchet of his prose-poetry; and catapulting great hunks of stony verbiage into them, so that the capitalists abandoned their cars and ran, screaming, tongues cleaved to the roofs of their mouths.

No. I resolved to walk to New York because I had business there, to explore; and, also, because in so doing, I hoped to suture up one of the wounds in my own,

divided psyche: to sew together my American and my English flesh, my mother's and my father's body bags, sundered by marriage, rived by death. And maybe even, at a more grandiose level (exhibiting what might be termed a Terroristic Personality Disorder), to expiate the sense of weird culpability that had dogged me, ever since 11 September 2001, when, returning from lunch with our then one-month-old youngest son, my wife, out of pure, journalistic reflex, snapped on the rolling news channel.

First we saw recorded footage of the North Tower being hit by American Airlines Flight 11; and then, seamlessly, live footage of the South Tower, as United Airlines Flight 175 punched a hole in its façade that had all the cartoon noir simplicity of Mickey Mouse's silhouette. Jaw slack, mind numb, I stared at the shaken-up snow globe of Manhattan for a while, then said to my wife: 'Well, there's nothing much I can do about this, I'm going upstairs to work.' Only to have her, twenty minutes later, shout up three storeys of our London house: 'Look! The whole building is collapsing, I really think you ought to be watching this!'

Indeed, I ought. And not to minimise my own part in it (how would this be possible?), things were not the same afterwards, for me, for the dead, the maimed and the traumatised, for Muslims, martyrs, Republicans, Jews and even journalists. So, I resolved to walk to New York in the spirit of peace, tracked lazily overhead, as I traversed west London, by the fat fuselages of the long procession of jets that caromed down the crystal hill of the flight path into Heathrow.

Could my own, slow advance, needle-limbs piercing and repiercing the fabric of reality, sew up this singularity, this tear in the space-time continuum through which medievalism had prolapsed? Legs slowing down . . . a trick-turning ape balancing the globe . . . slower and slower, then halting it altogether – a long fermata: serpentine, hairy arms bat at biplanes – before reversing it . . . walking backwards to roll back the years to some poorly imagined Arcadian past, where livestock, saints and the virginal abide by the Laws and a pleasing *sfumato* obscures everything.

On my walk to New York, passing through Wandsworth Park, which lies on the south side of the Thames, just before Putney Bridge, I was struck by the industrial blower mounted on the back of a small truck that was sending the old-gold autumnal leaves skittering away across the combed grass. This was like some hackneyed filmic symbol – the pages of a calendar torn off by invisible hands – used to denote the passage of time. And walking, too, blows back the years, especially in urban contexts. The solitary walker is, himself, an insurgent against the contemporary world, an ambulatory time traveller. The first time I walked to Heathrow Airport, I reached the road tunnel that plunges beneath the runways and into the terminal complex, only to find the following sign: 'No pedestrian access. Go back to the Renaissance.' This was, of course, a hotel on the Bath Road from where you are required to take a shuttle bus.

Yes, this was to be a peaceable protest, this discontinuous march from Stockwell in south London to the Lower East Side of Manhattan. If I was assaulting a tyranny

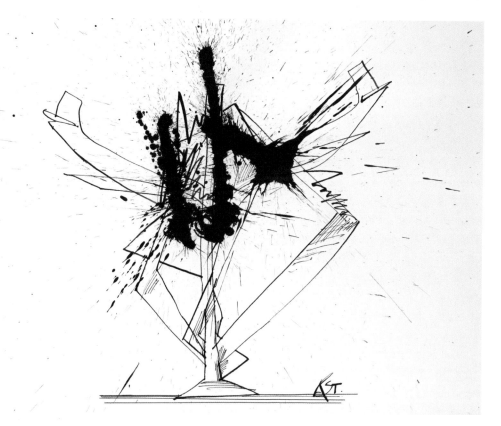

it was one of distance, and of a form of transportation that decentres and destabi-lises us, making all of us that can afford it subjects of a ribbon empire that encircles the globe. This is a papery and insubstantial realm, like a sanitary strip wrapped around a toilet bowl.

It's Wednesday, and I must be in Bangkok, Benin or Beijing, although not because I know in any meaningful sense *where* I am; for, if you were to take me outside this hotel, I'd be hard pressed to point north, let alone tell you what lay in that direction. When we marvel at the hermetic culture of the foreign bases, from which, sated by roast meals and entertained by imported TV shows, our fucked-up troops emerge to fuck up those who can't afford airline seats, we should rightly understand that we too belong to this army of disorientation, sallying forth from Holiday Inns and Hiltons, on missions of search & acquisition.

Bite down on this, why don't you? Bin Laden spoke of 9/11 as a 'spectacular', a horrid echo of Debord. And his terrorist affiliates – who applied to Al-Qaeda for venture capital, exactly like any other business start-up – weren't only attacking the Twin Towers as the supreme interfusion of capitalistic symbol and Western hege-monic reality, they were also attacking our transport system. Try to think of the civilians killed as collateral damage, as we do when we bunker-bust in Afghanistan and Iraq or our proxies do in the Lebanon and Somalia.

Even in England's own greening, our home-grown religious maniacs understood which form of transport was appropriate (as did the Moroccan Al-Qaeda freelanc-ers who wreaked pre-emptive vengeance on Madrid). They may have been led by a lowly classroom assistant, yet as they petted and aroused their new primitivism via the internet – self-grooming paedophiles, both corrupters and corrupted in a worldwide web of deception – there was this nascent awareness: that just as the Modernism of New York reached its apogee in the 1920s, with its pre-stressed steel and poured concrete buildings, so London's own, Modernist era was at the turn of the previous century: the soaring glass and iron rail terminuses, the deep-level Tube system augured through the clay of the Thames Valley. The 'spectaculars' of both 9/11 in New York and 7/7 in London were thus attacks on our notion of ourselves as, above all, a mobile society, ever stimulating our ever growing, ever more turgid economy with rapid movements of hand and eye.

They – that nebulous, shape-shifting 'other' – have remained faithful to this plan of attack. Nothing so static as a stadium or a queue for them, and into the summer of 2006, if the spooks are to be believed, they persisted with their evil designs on transatlantic flight. They won't let go of the possibility of pulling off a 'spectacular' to match their last. The bomb-making materials may have been mundane – hairspray, cleaning fluid, lighter fuel – but the blast would be anything but, tearing down tens – scores, even – of jets from the sky, thereby, simultaneously, thrusting the eastern seaboard away from the West Country, while yet, perversely, drawing them into tight, political proximity.

Still, if the spectacularists were intent on dividing and ruling, then they couldn't have done better. The seeming unanimity in the first, shocked months after 9/11 was just that. Soon enough, we began to 'other' each other.

The opposition to the retributive attacks on Afghanistan began quickly here in London. I was going to public meetings within days, and a local Stop the War coalition committee was set up. Attending this (in the upstairs hall of the local swimming baths, used typically for winter badminton and five-a-side soccer), I was struck by the juxtaposition between the platform apparatchiks and the masses. The latter were *rentiers* living off the consumer credit provided by their ever escalating property values; the former, the same rent-a-proles that I'd seen at leftist groupuscules a quarter-century before, right down to their Doctor Marten's boots; right up to their shop-worn rhetoric. When I addressed the meeting I said only this: that for every 'comrade' one of them uttered they could guarantee losing another hundred – or thousand – potential supporters.

It's only the benefit of hind-facetiousness that leads me to observe how queer it was that while these unrepentant Trotskyists were, with dull predictability, using one coalition as a front for their belated attempts to kick-start the permanent revolution, so their recusant brothers and sisters were the *éminences grises* behind another one; a coalition that, even as we fruitlessly deliberated, was kicking the chocks away from its B52s.

And so it went on: the grapes of wrath trailed across Afghanistan and Iraq, the bitter *vendage* of civilian deaths, then the hypostatisation of terror through the cirrhotic liver of another failed state. Yet, throughout all of this, what mattered most was the way we were divided: from our consciences, from our own, delusional sense of righteousness. As if the dreadful, old world of left and right were any less binary than this terrible new one? Both the best, the worst and – more importantly – the mediocre, lacked all conviction, while all three moieties were, nonetheless, full of passionate intensity.

What became clear to me in the short term was how wrong I'd been: at the back end of 2001, all the way through to March 2003, the numbers in Britain opposing the West's interventionism grew and grew. For every 'comrade' uttered at a swimming-pool meeting, a hundred more rushed to the colours, rallying beneath a burning Stars and Stripes. The climacteric came for me when a good friend told me

how he had wept with joy to see the flag of the USA set light to in Whitehall.

Now, hang on a minute, I thought: I'm an American. And ever since a little – and very understandable – contretemps with the black shirts of Homeland Security, as I was entering the States in 2002 (a trifling matter of drugs convictions), I had been compelled to activate my citizenship and travel to the US on a US passport. Yet even without this very personal goad, I like to think the sheer mirror-imaging of one array of Manicheans by another would have jibed, and made me realise that what was needed here was a little less ideology – not still more; a little less posturing about human rights and a little more hand-to-hand contact.

So much to heal with my feet: along with the semi-self-hatred of a demi-Jew, I now had the internecine conflict between my American and my English sides. Not that this was of a form that my parents would have understood, dying as they both had, before the spectacularists really got going. Nor was theirs a transatlantic marriage fraught by the way either of them pronounced 'either'. True, my father, towards the end of his own life, was subject to saying that my mother's might have been happier if she'd married 'a nice, little Jewish man', but I never remember him saying anything at all about the fact that his second wife was an American.

As for my mother, she was bipartisan in the extreme: opining at one and the same time that she loathed what the States had become politically, while never for a second dreaming of renouncing her citizenship; and, indeed, taking the trouble to ensure that my brother, Jonathan, and I would share it.

After she died, I found a letter in my mother's papers, apparently solicited by her from a cousin in Ohio. It's dated 1980 and this cousin writes that, on cleaning out his basement, he came upon a few books belonging to my great-grandfather. One of these, a prayer book published in Russia in 1883, had some Hebrew handwriting on its end papers. This, the cousin took the trouble to have translated.

It's slim pickings. Written in November 1919, on the first page my great-grandfather employs the Star of David as a device and writes in each section, thus: 'My name. This is. The ritual slaughterer Isaac son of Rabbi Yehuda Zalkind or Rosenbloom. Born in Villna.' The rest is a list of holy books the patriarch particularly favoured, some proverbs and a few terse remarks about his offspring. Isaac's second son, my grandfather, is glossed: 'My son Yaakov was born the day after Yom Kippur. It was a Tuesday at 6.00 in the morning. October 7, 1891. 24 Watrin Street [sic?], America.'

Why thanks, Isaac, that really hammers it down. It is almost as if you anticipated the topographical obsession of your descendant, and decided to utterly frustrate it. It's beautifully succinct, that address; expressing an ideation, I would say, as much as a location. In its way, my great-grandfather's imagining of America was as bald as any spectacularist's.

My mother spoke little of her childhood and was profoundly uneasy with her Jewishness. She denied ever having been bas mitzvahed – which was untrue. In retrospect, she was a typical, third-generation immigrant. At one time my mother implied that we were Poles, at another, Russians. Villna, certainly, is in Belarus. I suspect she either didn't know, didn't want to know, and maybe even didn't care. The 'Rosenbloom' was, so far as she was concerned, an insult; and being by nature a resentful person, she liked to dwell on this. She bought the old canard that this was a joke name, imposed on us by wiseacre Ellis Island officialdom, probably Irish-Americans. In due course my Uncle Bob changed his name to Ross.

From where did we come to New York? And, more importantly, how? I know not. Isaac writes: 'I left Romshishiak Falk Havana on September 11, 1888. I came to America November 26, 1888 on Wednesday.' Is this a progression of places: Romshishiak – Falk – Havana, as Joyce summed up his itinerary for the 1900s: 'Trieste – Zurich – Paris'? The timing would seem to suggest it. One thing is for certain: whatever his route, my great-grandfather didn't walk to New York.

# Walk One: Bucolic London

Enough. 7.30 a.m., Wednesday 29 November 2006. Coffee drunk, cigarette smoked, bowels evacuated, and I'm off, tiptoeing from the Victorian house in Stockwell where my wife and children are still abed. A four-storey, terraced house I've lived and written in this last decade, gradually cluttering up the locale with more and more narrative, on paper and in memory.

I'm keyed up as I head off along the road; the sky behind the block of flats ahead is cloudless and still a paving-stone grey; yet it brightens from pace to pace – the day will be clear. I'm conscious that even if I'll only be gone a matter of days I will not return from the walk to New York the same man. I shall have learnt something. Paul Theroux writes, in *The Great Railway Bazaar*, of sliding past the backs of London houses, as the first train of many carries him off. At the foot of the railway embankment properly settled lives are piled – cucumber frames and washing lines effulgent in the morning sunlight – while with each click-clackety mile, the writer becomes more exiguous, more of an observer.

But here, in Stockwell, striding down to the Wandsworth Road and working my way through the red-brick blocks of the interwar, London County Council flats, I'm still heavily embodied. The hydrocephalic brow of Lambeth College – a building of surpassing ugliness, Brutalism as deformity – has featured in one of my stories, as has this very route, set down – if not exactly immortalised – in another of my tales, 'The Five Swing Walk'.

I have limned then hymned the fly-tipped garbage at the bottom of these flats: the Stella Artois boxes, crushed picnic chairs, torn-out MDF kitchen units and garish plastic toys – even the swollen gonads of the humped, black rubbish bags. I have meditated upon our local equivalents of a catafalque – angle irons sprouting from brick, strung with barbed wire and steel mesh, webbed with polythene – more times than I care to think. Oft times London is a heavy coffin, borne upon such security ornamentation.

The wholesale fruit and vegetable market at Nine Elms is stirring, diesels cough and splutter. Casual workers – Kosovan, by the looks of them – clamber over the wall and down on to a vertically aligned pallet. They've come a long way from the Balkans to take this short cut through the Patmore Estate. They limp off ahead of me between the chequerboard blocks along Thessaly Road. I walk the children to Battersea Park down this road, I cycle this way if I am going anywhere in the west of London. Always, the small parade of shops beneath the last block of flats has struck me as the saddest, the most miserable encrustation of commerce: FF Foodfare, Better Buys of Battersea, Thessaly Newsagents – stinky little caves full of tomato soup, sugar and cut-price alcohol.

Now, the encrustation has been crushed. A month ago a crane working on the adjacent building site collapsed on to these flats. A local man, Michael Alexa, aged twenty-three, was killed washing his car. The pathos of this: the off-duty bus driver, soaping the flanks of his motor one second, the next – according to a local resident – 'It was like he'd been pushed into the windscreen, and the crane had gone right through him.' The crane operator was also killed. The flats are now knock-kneed and condemned; the end of the building has been roughly truncated. In the gutter are stooks of faded flowers in cellophane funnels, together with handwritten condolence cards: the wayside shrine of contemporary folk religion.

Barratt Homes – whose crane did for the bus driver – are putting up new apartments here in anticipation of the redevelopment of Battersea Power Station. Sir Giles Gilbert Scott's behemoth dominates this quarter of London – perhaps, psychically, the entire city. The footprint of the building is larger than Trafalgar Square;

the main turbine hall could engulf Wren's St Paul's, dome and all. Its distinctive, inverse-pool-table shape squats on the beer-soaked pub carpet of the London sky, yet for almost a quarter-century now the hulk has been hollowed out: an awesome shell of a Modernist ruin.

While the old Power Station *could* engulf St Paul's, it does eat developers. There's something cheering in the way it gobbles them up. First it was Robert McAlpine, the construction tycoon and Tory Party Treasurer, and now the Hwangs, the brothers who run Park, a Hong Kong-based property consortium, have been ingurgitated. They were bruiting their plans about town for a while: they were going to stuff the hulk with luxury flats, multiplex cinemas, design studios, hotels, conference centres and restaurants. Ah, restaurants! When the Hwangs' PR flak took me round the sight, we went up on to the roof and he pointed to the top of one of the signature chimneys: 'There's going to be a circular restaurant in there,' he said. 'The most exclusive in London, only sixteen diners, round a single table accessed by a lift.'

The only thing that got eaten was his bosses. The costs mounted. The Power Station is built from thousands upon thousands of courses of muddy London bricks. It's as close to a Babylonian ziggurat as any twentieth-century building could be. The mortar between these bricks perished during the Power Station's working life. As it's a listed building, any developers are under an obligation to preserve its fabric extant; and when they buy the building they all swear they will, even if it means repointing every single brick. But the truth is, you couldn't repoint Battersea Power Station even if you had every bricklayer in Romania to hand.

Now the Hwangs have flogged it to an Irish consortium, Treasury Holdings, and the new owners are making all the same noises they once did, little burps and lip smacks of developing satiety. A Council spokesman says, 'It's early days', but I say the table's already set in the chimney-top restaurant, and developer is on the menu.

The foolish purchasers of Barratt Homes' apartments – who promise on their billboards that prospective residents will be next to the most exciting new development in the city – will instead live out their mortgages confronted by this crumbling, acid-corroded behemoth.

So Battersea Power Station stands, as a dead weight, pinioning the Thames littoral. As I stride alongside it and look to the north-east, I see the glinting tiara of the London Eye Ferris wheel, poking above the jumble of warehouse units and the Cringle Dock Waste Management Centre. Beside the Eye are the golden finials of the Houses of Parliament: Walt Disney and Sir Walter Scott collaborate on a

fantasia of a democracy. The hoardings screening off the foreground of the Power Station are plastered with tag lines: 'A is for Art', 'F is for Fashion', 'H is for Homes' – such inspiring remedial instruction.

In Battersea Park a few commuters are hurrying along the gravel paths and pot-holed roadways. The gondola that adverts the Gondola Café is heeled over in the muddy waters of the boating lake. On the far shore rises the rockery, where my smaller children like to clamber in teensy ravines choked with empty beer cans. So the sublime ends. I work my way down through the glades and avenues, a Victorian conception of a municipal garden-for-all, imposed atop this old shambles where once gypsies camped and knackers boiled horses' corpses down for glue.

It's always thus: the first few hours of a long walk out of London. Gummed up with memories and referentia, my very psyche not only feels sticky – but thickening by the yard. It occurs to me that if I am akin to any literary traveller, it's Laurence Sterne, oscillating in the moment, dizzied by impressions and unable to make it from the remise door to the Calais Inn, let alone progress into France and Italy.

23

A recent re-landscaping of the Park has raised hillocks; grassy lipomas curve parenthetically around new public toilets that are, themselves, modishly curvilinear and walled with glass bricks. Winter pansies flare in serried ranks. Yet to my eye the ornamental troughs filled with scuzzy water, the boxy shrub holders decorated with sheet metal cut into flame shapes and the circlets of flagpoles, are more present. No tumulus nouveau can obscure these: the remnants of the old Battersea Funfair that I revered as a child.

A school friend's tenth birthday party. His father drove us down here from Highgate in his E-Type Jaguar. The father and his two sons – all three had tight globes of curly hair; Jewfros, you might say. He gave all us kids a fifty pence coin to spend – shocking largesse; the pentagonal heft of the novelty currency, sharp in my hand. I couldn't wait to spend it on the Watersplash ride. I wasn't surprised when, a quarter-century later, this cool, beneficent dude emerged as one of the chief benefactors of Tony Blair's New Labour.

Or fazed by *The Day the Earth Caught Fire*, a British sci-fi film, made in the year of my birth, which swam on to TV during my dopey years in the late seventies. The protagonists are on the rollercoaster at Battersea Funfair when the Thames transmogrifies into a sheet of flame. A joint of Moroccan hash and hokey special effects – what could be finer? And now? Why, the parallax of time – which draws formerly distant events into tight proximity – has quite as much force as the nuclear tests that, in the film, push the earth from its axis and send it careering towards the sun. 1961, then 1971, now 2006 – the futuristic lineaments of the 1950s Funfair withstand the passage of the decades, while all about them insect joggers buzz and blip.

I recall the summer of 1989, and the wedding of some friends held in the lee of the Peace Pagoda, at that time a new and startling structure, like the Albert Memorial squatted in by four svelte Buddhas. I remember – what seemed to me – a rancorous speech by the bride's father. I put a version of it into my novella, *Cock*. Then it's a decade later, and I'm lifting one of my kids up on to the top tier of the Pagoda, so he or she can consort with the Prince of Non-Attachment. It was raining, a Parks Police car came sidling up the avenue and one of the cops hailed us through a megaphone: 'Get down off the Buddha!'

Now, proceeding, I see over there the little plantation of trees beside Albert Bridge. My friend John McVicar, once the most wanted man in Britain – latterly not much wanted at all, so he moved to Bulgaria to hunt wild boar – planted a tree here for his late mother. It would've been in the mid-1990s. Could it be that inapposite conifer, the quick green fuse of which lances through cast-iron railings?

Below the Thames unrolls the smooth production line of its ebb tide, upon which are bolted together garbage scows heading down from Wandsworth.

Perhaps. Oscar and Jimmy walk on the far side of the river, plotting nocturnes, proleptically graffiti-spraying butterflies. Over towards Chelsea shines the single, gold ball atop the Chelsea Harbour development. This was the motif – the ball rises and falls with the tide, like a ball cock in a cistern – with which I opened my 1997 novel *Great Apes*. Chelsea Harbour, an integrated development of luxury flats and costly retail outlets. Think gym, think gated, think Eurotrash. Michael Caine had a restaurant here – perhaps he still does – certainly, it would be fair to say that his entire acting career led up to this imposture. The chirpy Cockney rhymer: 'My name is 'arry Palmer, I run a restaurant in Chelsea 'arbour.'

In his 2001 novel *Millennium People* J.G. Ballard made an apocalyptic dystopia of Chelsea Harbour, wreathing the ugly pagoda of its central tower with the smoke from the Volvos and Range Rovers set on fire by its revolting tenants: bored, nihilistic bourgeois; spectacularists seeking some vivification in violence. I now realise, on this very walk, that Jim has made this Thames littoral his own. Not that he really cares about London per se, although, looked at another way, he is the purest psychogeographer of us all, ever dissolving the particular and the historical in the transient and the psychic. Making states into states of mind. From Terry Farrell's spec office block – now occupied by the Secret Service – to Chelsea Harbour, and on upriver, the last fifteen years have seen a great and glassy burgeoning of these – Jim's mind children – 'luxury' developments. At first rectilinear and concrete, latterly faced with 'weathered' boards, to give them that authentic 'wharf' feel, the apartment blocks would be just as at home in Malmö or on the Mediterranean.

I won't get very far if memories, dreams and reflections continue to obscure this bright, late November morning. In the 1960s, even a decade after the Clean Air Act, I can still remember there being London 'particulars' so thick we had to feel our way along the privet hedges back home from the Tube station. These are cloudy memories of a foggy past, but all is clear on the embankment beside Lord Norman Foster's atelier; even at this hour young architects are a'CADing, and through the white graticule of the blind I can see neat, white models of towns, plotted in wood and plastic. These are graphic, apprehensible, unlike the two-millennia-old moraine I'm struggling across.

Thankfully, past Battersea Bridge things clear a little. I'm gathering pace and breasting the ebb tide of commuters walking, jogging and cycling along the riverside path. I am the reverse commuter, for while they head from the suburbs into the city centre, I pack my briefcase and walk to work on the periphery; it's there

that I stake my claim, mine my words. I'm gathering pace – and satisfactorily losing definition. Soon I'll be Ballardian myself, my name a prosaic Anglo-Saxon puzzle – Vaughan, Ventriss, Laing – which, even when solved, will tell you only my profession and my class.

But at St Mary's, Battersea, a perfect jewel of a late eighteenth-century church, I'm derailed once more. A stiletto steeple stabs up from this solid yet airy building. At the foot of the small, irregular churchyard, the barges of urban shedonists are permanently moored; while all around mount the gleaming bluffs of still more luxury apartments. Somewhere inside these there are dot-com start-up millionaires, smearing on lube and despair, whereas inside St Mary's, 220-odd years ago, William Blake married Catherine Boucher, the daughter of a local market gardener. She signed the register with an unenigmatic 'X'. Blake – what would he have made of walking to New York? Blake, of whose work it's been said: this is what a bad artist would produce if he were to be a genius.

I see the church door is open – it's always been locked when I've passed this way before – so I enter, to hear the creed intoned by a crop-headed curate: 'Glory be to the Father, and to the Son . . .' and then the whispered gentility of the all-female congregation's response. In the vestibule there are handy umbrellas to keep these dry communicants still drier. The church's interior is as expected: manila envelopes lain out for donations, jam jars containing weedy specimens, and a dangling chandelier as organic as a beehive. This is the desiccated diminuendo of the Church of England; what began in the moist rage of paterfamilias manqué is ending with a little parched glory for the (absent) father.

I think Blake would've depicted the walk to New York thus: with me a small figure, crushed beneath the dead weight of the blue sky, while across this loose swathe the fuselages of the aircraft coming in to land at Heathrow are struggling to separate from one another, like the proto-Muybridge, time-lapse etchings that the bad genius made of angels and human traffic. The nose cones of 747s and airbuses stretched apart, between them stria of ectoplasm, time-goo.

At Battersea Reach the riverbanks draw back. Think Rotterdam, and the kindergarten Cubism of Dutch contemporary architecture, yet bowdlerised still further by the cost considerations of these London developers, the complacent edificers of Kingfisher and Oyster wharves. The world is getting hotter; hotter right here as I head inland, sopping up monoxide as I circumambulate the gyroscopic advertising hoarding that dangles above the roundabout at the end of Wandsworth Bridge. Maybe I should buy the Navman sat-nav advertised on a fly-poster, a snip at £149.99, inclusive of free set-up and demo? With a satellite navigation system, I need never again inhabit the physical world; I can simply look from dash-mounted screen to windscreen and back again, as I drive – on instrumentation alone – from my office workstation to my domestic entertainment system. What a blessed relief.

Blessed relief from Jew's Lane and the gnomon of a lamp-post, its hard shadow lying across a cycle path, defined by paint as thick as toothpaste. Blessed relief from the old London brick of a Fuller's pub, that's advertised, bizarrely, by a sign depicting a giant hand picking up an ocean-going liner. London Pride – that's Fuller's finest tipple. In my drinking days I had plenty of it – pride, that is. Blessed relief from the Wandsworth waste depot: yellowy container-loads of composted shit, blood and obsolete electrical goods, being winched out over the river, then down on to barges, that in turn will be pushed through the twisting colon of the Thames, downriver.

Here, the Wandle, one of London's lost rivers, joins the Thames. Two years ago, in the summer, I turned left at this fluvial junction and followed its course upstream, past William Morris's wallpaper factory at Merton and Lady Hamilton's house. A female psychogeographer, if ever there was one, Emma diverted the Wandle to run through her grounds, and dubbed it 'the Nile' in honour of her lopsided squeeze. I went on, past where the Wandle rises at Carshalton, thence to Croydon, thence up and on to the North Downs, where, at a curious feature called the Norr Chalk Pinnacle, I could see the entire lower valley of the Thames spread out before me: the flybuzz of aircraft circling over Heathrow, the tiny minarets of the city, the Jew's harp of the Queen Elizabeth II Bridge, vibrating at Dartford.

I plodded on, down into the Surrey weald, up into the Ashdown Forest, down into the Sussex weald and up again on to the South Downs. I didn't stop until I reached Newhaven on the south coast, three days after I'd quit the Thames. I've

27

been doing this for a few years now: stepping from my London house and stalking a hundred miles or so into the hinterland. In middle age I no longer want to know where I'm going – only where I've been all these years.

This summer I walked from where I live now, to where I was born, to where I grew up, to where I was at school, to where I was at university. Stockwell – Charing Cross – Hampstead Garden Suburb – Finchley – Oxford. My own Trieste – Zurich – Paris, the itinerary of an internal exile. When I was a teenager I assumed that I'd travel – and far. Then my father emigrated, my mother died and my brothers moved abroad, while I remained here, in London. Now I realise I never wanted to travel at all, simply get away from – what psychotherapeutic geographers dub – my Family of Origin. How good of them to leave me in vacant possession of an entire metropolis, so that I could furnish it with my own memories, dreams and reflections.

The steely façades of the riverfront blocks are now warm to the touch, and builders and tradesmen are stripped to their T-shirts. I left Stockwell in cagoule and cashmere pullover, but as I gain Putney Bridge I strip to my own T-shirt and sit at a zinc-topped table outside a branch of Carluccio's, sipping a latte and eating an almond pastry. Inside the décor is scrubbed, shining. Cheeses, salamis, potted pimentos – they all crackle beneath cellophane and strip lighting. I've met Carluccio himself on a couple of occasions; he's a friend of a friend. Here he is, on the cover of one of his cookery books, which is propped up on a central display table underneath a dwarf Christmas tree. *Antonio Carluccio Goes Wild*. He carries a wooden truckle full of tasty herbage; he looks rubicund and happy – not feral at all.

Yes, Jim Ballard was right. The public spaces of London are becoming outdoor atria, retail boulevards servicing Mediterranean-style business parks. Patrick Keiller, on the other hand, was wrong. The melancholia that infuses his epic and elegiac 1991 film, *London*, has been blown away – like the leaves in Wandsworth Park – by an airy consensus: nothing succeeds like excess. It's easier for those of my generation, coming to our majority in the dog days of the early 1980s, to embrace a city in permanent decline. The desuetude and neglect of public spaces is filmic, while the camera lens simply reflects itself in mirrored buildings.

I sit reading my wife's column in the *Independent*. She's anatomised the grisly aftermath of the stabbing of Tom ap Rhys Price, a young solicitor who was murdered in Kensal Rise, north London. His killers have been shown extraordinary compassion by the victim's mother, who has decided to set up a charity to aid such disadvantaged inner-city black kids. I'm still in touch with the mother ship, linked

28

by mobile phone, so I text her my congratulations on her piece as I continue on up the Putney shore, past the boathouses where jolly, hefty girls, shrink-wrapped in Lycra, carry sculls down the slope to the lapping waves.

It's time to part from Father Thames – I'll meet him again at Richmond Bridge. I turn aside from the river and take a diagonal traverse across Putney Common. My mobile phone rings – it's my ex-wife. She needs to talk about our teenage son: he's indolent and stumbling about in the hazy realm of late adolescence. What to say? At his age I was intellectually omnivorous, true, but I was also teaching myself to shoot up smack. I think he's doing just fine; he's charming, funny and personable. But that's not the point: this phone call, this fishing line, lands me in the reticulation of my responsibilities. I thrash there as I plod through coverts and cross over sports pitches. I'm in Shepherds Bush – not Putney. I'm in my life, clamped in my persona, not the ghost in London's machine I fervently wish to be.

I'm unable to lose myself again until I break the connection, then find myself at the junction of the Upper Richmond Road and Priory Lane. I resist the urge to divert into memories of ill-advised sex with a girl from Sheen. It was daytime in her girlhood bedroom . . . I was shocked by the thick hairs sprouting from the aureoles of her dirigible breasts . . . No. Priory Lane runs up ahead of me, I have a rendezvous to make at Richmond Bridge by noon. If I come this way at all, to this outer suburbia, hard against Henry VIII's hunting ground, it's only to visit friends banged up in the private psychiatric hospital, the Priory. The Priory – notorious, it is. Notorious not least because its millionaire owner, Dr Chai Patel, is bound up in the cash-for-honours scandal that is, predictably, darkening still more the dying days of the Blair regime.

And notorious also for its celebrity clientele: the jittery cokehead models and smacked-about rockers, who gabble and purge in its addiction unit. The Priory: such a cliché that there's already been a chat show on British TV called *The Priory*. The Priory, a fine, large, Gothic-revival house that already by 1876 was being gazetted thus: 'Built for the late Lord Justice Sir J. Knight Bruce, it is now a private lunatic asylum.' Indeed, yes. I've been here to visit, to sit with desolate friends on its sickly lawns, beneath its magnolia faux-battlements. Or, on provision of an exeat, to wander with these saddos in Richmond Park, anatomising how it can be that their lives have been so dismembered.

But, before I reach the environs of the Priory, I'm struck by a mean little breezeblock parade of shops, stuck in the arse end of a 1980s development. 'St Marcus' reads the sign on the largest of these, 'S.A. Minimart, Biltong and Boere Wors'. Intrigued, I go in, to find myself surrounded by what look like flattened bulls' pizzles, dangling from steel rails. Signs at one end of these rails read 'Hard End', at the other 'Soft'. These are, perforce, strips of biltong – the sign didn't lie. This has to be the biggest biltong emporium in the northern hemisphere. There are hundreds of strips of the stuff: chilli-flavoured biltong, garlic biltong, biltong flavoured any number of ways. How many hard-masticating South Africans must London contain in order to support this minimart full of beef jerky?

The great wonder of my adult life – a desultory period, 1979–2006, all are agreed, no Blitz only bits of this and that, epochs of haircuts – has been the cosmopolitanisation of London. The three hundred languages spoken on the streets of the city; the rise in the ethnic minority population from 7 per cent to 25 per cent; the minicab drivers more familiar with Conkary than the Cally Road; and these strips of biltong are part of that, a sinewy girdle about the globe. I buy one to gnaw on, washed down with Evian, as I foot it up Priory Lane, through Roehampton Gate and into the park.

Which I've never liked, really. Never liked its trees, artificially grouped: Yikes! I want to cry, here comes the copse! The last day of November and the leaves are still on the oaks and beeches, mellow gold and brown as Old Holborn hand-rolling tobacco. Beneath this canopy lie artily deposed trunks, strewn about on the tawny sward. Their bark stripped by the deer, they're like the toppled torsos in some de Chirico dreamscape.

Bertrand Russell grew up here, in one of the capacious lodges. A mean-spirited childhood with emotionally retarded grandparents deranged by snobbery and their proximity to power. Think cold winter walks, crackling over hoarfrost in scratchy tweed knickerbockers. Think mortification of the bowels with lumps of suet. No wonder the weedy kid plotted to reduce language to a series of logical formulae. Poor little fucker.

I've never liked Richmond Park's contrived ambience of the farouche – a centuries' old shtick. The scale of Richmond Park is wrong: people come here to drive about in their SUVs and look at the deer, and, in fairness, this being the time of the annual cull – the deer, that is, not the people – they are in great numbers, the stags photogenically tossing their antlers. But if an SUV in central London is a solecism, here in the park it's an insult. The local council certainly think so – they've become the first in London to levy a special tax on the hypertrophied all-terrain baby-buggies, the Porsche Cayennes and Volkswagen Touaregs. Vehicles, I was told recently, that are known to cognescenti as 'badge cars'. Henry VIII would have approved. I picture him hunting deer armed with a 9mm Glock pistol, from the front seat of his Land Rover Vogue. He is impersonated by Ray Winstone, who, on cornering his prey, snarls: 'Gotcha, you filfy littul toerag . . .'

I gain the crest of the hill and there it is, falling away behind me, swags and ruches of greenery and brick, under the blue-painted ceiling of its recent conversion: New London, city of the toppermost property prices. I can see a golden drop of sunlight on the glans of the Swiss Re Tower (Lord Foster's phallus, commonly known as the Gherkin), and the inverted pool table of Battersea Power Station. I can see the Hampstead massif and the Telecom Tower. I can see my life, entire, in a single saccade.

Then I go over the top, past the Royal Star and Garter Home, a redbrick semi on steroids with neoclassical breast implants. Below me the Terrace Gardens fall away, beyond them Petersham Meadows and then the river again, boats moored in mid-stream. The Thames shines bright between wooded banks that are deceptively countrified. I trudge down Richmond Hill, past the kind of shops my mother would have damned as 'chi-chi' – although not without a trace of envy. Where did she get all this snobbery from? True, she attended Richmond Hill High School herself. But I thought that was Richmond Hill on Long Island. Did they anticipate Nancy Mitford there? Was every particular divided into U and Non-U? Expressions my mother also coveted as her own.

Mediterraneo, The Gooday Gallery (in this stands a man, wearing a shirt, the entire back of which is the more comely front of Botticelli's Venus), Natural Flooring, a florist called The Wild Bunch, a kids' clothing store dubbed Neck and Neck. After she died, in the neurotic sediment of her diaries and journals – forty years of minutely described sexual obsession and phobia – I found lists of these: 'The Mane Event', 'Hair Today'; punning retail concerns had preoccupied her. Why, Mother? Oh, why?

At Richmond Bridge the Riverside development is to my right: a grotesque confabulation of old and new-tricked-out-as-old. The nineteenth-century town hall, the eighteenth-century Heron House, Laxton's 1856 Italianate Tower House – all have been soldered together by an awful mucilage of Georgian-cum-Palladian office bollix, complete with cupolas and columns aplenty. Nine thousand nine hundred square metres of office space in all, falling down to the river in series of terraces; grassy ghats upon which the bourgeoisie should rightfully be burnt alive for sanctioning such ugliness at all. It's courtesy of the 'architect' Quinlan Terry, natch, pseudo-artificer by appointment to Chucky 'HRH' Windsor, who would doubtless concur with his protégé that 'Modernism is a sign of the fall from grace'.

It's suitable that this – my first and last Thames crossing – should be mediated on the one hand by Our Tel and on the other by the bridge itself: five pure spans, rendered in Portland stone, completed in 1777, it's the oldest in the burgh. London – as has been remarked – was only a Modernist city a hundred years ago. Ever since, it's been in steady flight from the present, putting on its airbrakes with an anguished howl, landing on the short airstrip provided by a ha-ha, in an imagined, Arcadian past.

And there, standing in the middle of the bridge, as if detached from his own rather less Arcadian past, wearing a khaki anorak and sporting a woolly watch cap, a canvas army surplus rucksack on his shoulder, an Ordnance Survey map poking from his pocket, is Nick Papadimitriou, waiting to walk with me the last nine miles to Heathrow. Nine miles that will take us through territory he knows well: Twickenham and Hounslow Heath, where he botanises and meditates, Feltham, where he did time in borstal. Further on is the site of the new Terminal 5, formerly the Bedfont Court Estate, which Nick has hymned in his own writings as a lost Arcadia of municipal smallholdings. Here, at Richmond Bridge, and then, as we walk down the embankment footpath beside Marble Hill Park, my very different land marches with Nick's.

Initially, I can't quite connect with Nick. I'm still lost in my own reveries; shitty little memories. In the year before I finally quit drink and drugs, I struggled – like the quadriplegic I then was, all four limbs withered by decades of inanition – to get going. I couldn't yet counsel the notion of actually taking steps, so I flirted with wacky forms of transport. One of these was a Go-Ped, a tiny scooter with a 22cc engine tacked on to it. For a while, officialdom could not even apprehend these oddities, and I caromed about town on mine, to score on the corner of Oakley Street in Chelsea.

A maroon Ford Mondeo, the dealer at the wheel. He styled himself 'Andy', but we all knew his real name was Anand. Two of white, one of brown. Dropped from his mouth into my palm. Wife and kids away for the weekend – out of sight is out of mind for junkies. Hell, *in sight* is also out of mind. But I couldn't just get stoned any more; there was too much guilt, denial wasn't a river in Egypt any more, it was the Wandle, diverted through my own back garden.

So, I got loaded and drove my Go-Ped along the river to Richmond, believing this to be a healthy outing. All the way, on a hot summer's day, sweating through Mortlake, annoying families with its ghastly whine. I gave up at Our Tel's dreadful Riverside uglification and took a black cab home. Pity poor me. Inward bound, or as my family had every reason to scream: 'Duck! Incoming fuckwit!'

More than a decade earlier I had held the implausible job title of 'Senior

Playleader', and worked at the adventure playground in Marble Hill Park. It was run by the Greater London Council, which held suzerainty over great swathes of the city's parkland. But that was then; like the evanescent empire of Alexander the Great, the GLC – London's only citywide governmental body – had disappeared, banished by Thatcher, the Finchley demagogue. The only relevant continuum, between 1985 and 1999, was my own smack habit.

I can see the adventure playground as Nick and I walk beside the river, past the implausible bashes of what must be river gypsies, longhairs with weedy tresses, temporarily run aground. See it, but it looks run down, in all probability by the local authority that took it over when the GLC folded. Adventure playgrounds – a peculiarly London phenomenon; the kinder-torture-gartens of the Blitz, established on bomb sites in the 1950s. They were always harum-scarum places, the apparatus toshed together out of railway sleepers and sections of telegraph poles. Six-inch nails planted in them, rusty hooks to catch urban sprats.

I loved them when I was a kid – the kids I supervised in the mid-1980s loved them quite as much, but they couldn't survive the safety industry, oh no. An industry still nascent on the baking afternoon in July 1985, when I left the kids and the rest of the staff, grouped round a black and white TV, and in the full, ruddy colour of my VW Scirocco GTi (given to me by a wealthy friend, later sold for an ounce of cocaine), drove at speeds well in excess of 80 mph, back to the flat in Kensington that was another part of the same friend's largesse. While 1.5 billion people in one hundred countries  watched – live! – Midge Ure yodel 'Oooooh, Vienna!' I had a hit of smack, and then drove back out to Marble Hill, all in under an hour.

There was a retarded kid called Phil – now, I daresay, he'd have special needs, but then he ran, roaring, around the adventure playground, a great lummox in a duffel coat, even on the hottest afternoons, bellowing at the other kids, who screamed and taunted. Care in the community was afforded both of us. Happy days, no?

Nick and I pass by Marble Hill House, a delightful Palladian villa built for some kingly mistress or another. Pope visited, Walpole visited – I've never been in. But then I've been to Agra and not the Taj Mahal, Grenada and not the Alhambra. Addiction can do that to you, clamp on the brick-wall blinkers so that for decades you trot around in circles, wherever you may be. I've awoken now, in my forties, to find myself in an unexplored sylvan glade. Is it any wonder I can't stop pacing forwards?

Actually, thank the gods for Nick, because this internal monologue is getting too jittery and too involved: a convolvulus of fact, memory and fancy; a palimpsest rubbed up out of smudged and scarred neurones. My feet are tangling up in its denim warp and cheesecloth weft. Let's tune out – and tune in again. These are the topics Nick addresses as we draw abreast of Eel Pie Island – implausible epicentre of the British blues revival of the 1960s – then deviate from the Thames into Church Street, Twickenham – where I have a beef sandwich on brown, and Nick a prawn on white – then tread on along Heath Road.

Timothy Leary, was he entirely bogus? Can there be any equivalence between mystical ecstasy and psychotropic drug experiences? Corvid intelligence, is it wholly unknowable? Environmental anxiety – the tendency people now have to react to any untoward weather with cries of 'It's global warming' – is this, in fact, a projection of other, more perennial anxieties? Frothy rivers in London – why do they froth? Nick's resounding affection for Philip Larkin's *The Whitsun Weddings* – 'I thought of London spread out in the sun / Its postal districts packed like squares of

wheat . . .' That 1970s anachronism – or so it seems to Nick, who finds his tolerance for the *niqab* and imported theocracy fast declining – 'No Platform for Racists or Fascists'. A murder in Barnet – or rather, several, for he's working on a book cataloguing them: an Edwardian, gay *crime passionnel* on the East End Road in Finchley; illiterate throwback tramps hacking each other to death on in 1930s Edgware; a 1950s gangland shootout in Finchley High Road; the skeletons of numerous babies found buried in the garden of a house in East Finchley at the turn of the nineteenth century.

Nick is, to be frank, irrepressible. He is a walking compendium of fact, opinion and supposition: a great Blue Nile of verbiage, that, when it's diverted to mingle with my own thoughtful tributary, completely alters its hue. He's good to walk with and, over twenty years now, we've done a few together. Too few, because in those two decades there have been many long hiatuses: Nick shivering for aeons on suburban station platforms, paralysed on his way to hit on suspicious chemists for codeine linctus, a purloined volume of experimental poetry digging into his hip; and me, another of the seven suburban sleepers, slumbering in some numb, tarry cul-de-sac.

So, thus engaged, we walk along Heath Road, a curving interwar shopping parade, with its mansard roofs and snotty rendering. Past the Twickenham Green Baptist Church, a startling folly: the Gothic envisioned by Orwell's Gordon Comstock. Hard by it there's a small shop selling Star Wars costumes. Darth Vader's head sits, unceremoniously, on a shelf. It's a snip, at £350, this creepy sci-fi chimera: part gas mask, part Samurai-cum-Nazi helmet. Nick and I are a long time ago in a galaxy far, far away, here on the outer rim of Twickenham.

We grew up within a couple of miles of each other, on the northern section of this particular London layer. For the city is like a tree, growing ring after ring of brick and privet. An expert – a London dendrochronologist, if you will – can assay precisely the period of the ring he's penetrating, and tell you what other 'burbs lie within it; thus: Twickenham, Isleworth, Brentford, Ealing, Wembley, Hendon, Finchley, and so on, round to Mitcham and Merton. We even turn off the Staines Road on to a 'Meadway', a grassy little avenue of semis exactly like the 'Meadway' in the Finchley suburb where I grew up.

And then we turn off this and along the banks of the River Crane, a surprisingly fast-flowing little rill. The Crane loops south here, although eventually it will turn north and, after being fed through the charcoal tanks of the sewage works at Isleworth, join the Thames. This, perhaps, is the hardest thing to explain about the walk to New York: bucolic London. 'You walked to Heathrow?' people will ask me in succeeding weeks. 'Wasn't that awfully grim? I mean, didn't you have to slog along the hard shoulder of the A4?' And then I tell them: 'Oh no, you don't understand, probably only four of the seventeen-odd miles were on roads at all, the rest . . .' are like this: the babbling brook, the damp tongue of leaf-pressed tarmac snaking through the grass, the sentinel yews and tipping rowans, the massy oaks still in leaf.

Palisade and picket fences run along the house backs, grubby greenhouses and rusty climbing frames clash in the gardens; then, as we penetrate further into the Nature Reserve, banks of brambles and nettles boil up and the path becomes a muddy slough wending along the riverbank. Up ahead looms the brick, oasthouse-shape of the Shot Tower, where shot was manufactured in the nineteenth century; globules of molten lead plummeting into deadly spheroids. Somewhere beyond this little lost world we can hear the tedious plaint of an ambulance siren.

Nick is entirely at home here, secure in this neglected and underimagined inter-zone. From time to time he will go into minor ecstasies over a manhole cover, a concrete sluice, or other evidence of interwar, riverine infrastructure. By the Shot Tower a great convocation of ring-necked parakeets are eee-chew-chew-chattering in an ash overrun with ivy. Their bottle-green and iridescent blue markings are dull in the gathering cloud of mid-afternoon. Alien interlopers, exotic escapees from garden aviaries: like other economic migrants they have gravitated towards the airport.

The Crane twists and splits; from piffling islets dangling branches scratch at its syrupy surface, snagging tendrils of polythene and discarded crisp packets. Along the banks great hanks of bramble are interspersed by the mighty umbels of Caucasian Giant Hogweed, another interloper, a vicious Triffid of a plant, mas-querading as cow parsley with a pituitary disorder. This is the landscape at once of my childhood and the futuristic dystopia of Ham in my novel *The Book of Dave*. The stems of the hogweed contain a photoactive poison; if you touch them and then are exposed to sunlight, painful blisters form full of gleet. Nick shows me the hogweed scars on his hands – nothing is really safe, boys may dabble in the brooks of childhood, yet the uncanny lurks in the maw of a foot tunnel jaggy with aerosol graffiti.

This is why the Russian Andrei Tarkovsky remains my favourite film director, and has been since I was twelve. His films are full of locations such as this: unmade environments, discombobulations of the urban and the rural. His favoured leit-motif is rain falling *inside* a building, a suspension of natural law that is curiously mundane. He is a refusenik – of dialectical materialism, and of all simple, lin-ear progressions, such as time, or narrative commonly understood. His prevailing mood is one of déjà vu: the uncanniness of sudden familiarity.

Neuroscience tells us that déjà vu occurs most frequently in adolescence for this reason: as the two sides of the brain finally begin to fuse, so the right 'recalls' what the left perceived only moments before. Yet Tarkovsky's films suggest that our memories of déjà vu are recollections of a precognition. So, we stand outside of time, here on the bank of the River Crane, Nick and I, our arms companionably linked in those of our adolescent selves, and look down at the plastic bottle, caught by an eddy, then pushed into a trough of virulent green algae. When did you first notice that Evian, backwards, spells naïve?

Then, at Baber Bridge we're out, back on the Staines Road, traffic swishes by a tyre shop staffed entirely by Asians. The suburban flatlands of north Feltham and Hatton stretch on either side of the road, mean bungalows and boarded-up pubs, a kebab hut styled 'Turkish Delight'. The Perspex bus shelters are brides scarified by knife-wielding bachelors. One scratched tag even reads 'FAKER'.

This is an environment leeched by the airport, which now we can hear, hollowly booming and howling in the near-distance, a black hole of internationalism, into which all the matter of outer London is sucked, only for it to emerge, sweaty and frowsty, in Stockholm or St John, Rio de Janeiro or Singapore. Yet the grey sky is curiously void of jets, the fat-bellied fowl that have flown with me all the way from Stockwell. Where are they? Waddling over yonder on their rubber wheels-for-webbed feet.

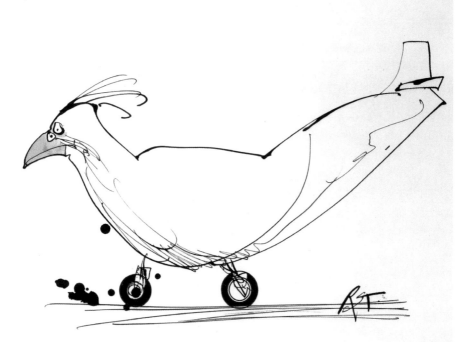

Nick is telling me about a man he knew when he was in an offenders' resettlement hostel in Cambridge. This man's great-grandfather was – or so he alleged – the last person in Britain to be hanged for cannibalism. As for Nick's friend, he shot and snared rabbits and expertly cooked them. Human–rabbit–chicken nugget, that's a meaty itinerary. Feral habits die hard on the road to deracination.

We turn off the Staines Road, cross a canal with the grandiose title 'The Duke of Northumberland's River', and pass by a school, alongside a scrubby field of allotments, that turns into a dirty pasture grazed by knock-kneed old tool sheds. It's four in the afternoon, and the kids are coming out of the chain-link gates, escorted by parents who look as if they might be the type to poke petrol-soaked rags through a paediatrician's letterbox.

Then, at last, at the end of Cain's Lane, we see it: the perimeter fence of Heathrow, and through its dull diamonds I can make out the tail fin of an intersuburban spaceship: 'United Airlines'. The last bungalow on Cain's Lane has a 1970s vintage white Cadillac parked outside of it, and in its front garden a mess of other, dismembered American cars. Can this, I wonder, be a harbinger of some kind?

Walking beside the Great South West Road is scary – heading up the slip road into Terminal 4 scarier still. We never knew how cosy the River Crane was until we found ourselves in this oily place, which repels us transparent, watery pedestrians. The sun has disappeared; the sweep of the grey-grassed embankments, the constriction of the knobbly concrete verges and the enfilades of dipping sodium lights that wade in them are all threatening. We are not wanted here, where there are no walkways, only forty-foot-high smiling Singaporean girls captioned: 'First to Fly the A380 from Heathrow'. We trip across elevated roundabouts and squeeze alongside crash barriers, ever wary for the pounce of cops or security guards; when Nick and I at last gain the terminal we're stressed out enough to find succour in a Starbucks tea and a bar of condensed muesli.

It's time for us to part. In under half an hour the whole, loose skein of the afternoon will have been unravelled for Nick, when the Heathrow Express deposits him in Paddington Station, to become once more a lonely wanderer in the sea of city folk.

# An Interlude: New-found-land

As for me, I check in and head through Security. They ask me if I mind having a full body scan, and I don't demur. Why would I? We all have to do our bit; the threat of terror induces in us all the desire to fulfil our civic duty of being permanently under suspicion. This is a strange, self-accusatory doublethink.

Unlacing my walking boots, I wait behind blue nylon bafflers for my turn to be zapped, idly inspecting a clipboard that notes the remarks of those who have declined the signal honour: 'Says she is pregnant', 'In a wheelchair', and the outrageous: 'Is it because I is black?' This last is a play upon the shtick of the north London comedian Sacha Baron-Cohen in his alter ego as Ali G., the most famous resident of the nearby suburb of Staines. That Ali G. is fictional only confirms the fact that Staines is an *unterburgh*.

I call over the Security man:

'That's an extremely stupid thing to leave in plain view,' I observe. 'Someone could get themselves into a lot of trouble.'

'You're not meant to read that!' he snaps, and snatches the clipboard from its peg.

'I read everything,' I say, quite as testily, 'I'm a journalist.'

Seconds later I find myself sky side, unscanned and wandering in my stockinged feet through the shiny, happy chancel of this Aeolian temple, past

Agent Provocateur, Harrods, Church's and Austin Reed. The England of prosperity-through-ever-rising-consumer-demand is here writ small and cloistered. Normally, on my long-distance walks, anoesis descends within a few miles: the mental tape loop of

infuriating resentments, or inane pop lyrics, or nonce phrases gives way to the greeny-beige noise of the outdoors. This time, however, the walk has been a clamber through a psychic lumber room; and it's only now, as I watch a Bloomberg news thread spool across a monitor, that I realise – or rather fail to – that I've finally tranced out.

What can be more null than these, the last few instants before an intercontinental flight, meted out by the unwanted drags on a necessitated cigarette? There are Swedes at the next table in the Ask bar; beyond them Hassidim in their silky coats hustle Samsonite luggage; still other religious sectaries – women, this time – trip by me with white napkins pinioned to their hair. I rouse myself to stump along through this un-place and experience beneath my now weary feet the passive, feline sag of the travelator. Then the last, scuffed yards of corrugated corridor, then the last frayed strip of red and yellow duct tape.

In the upper cabin of the British Airways jumbo, secreted in my pod, I call a friend in London and tell him of my great achievement. He laughs: 'Funny, you and Gaddafi both.' I ask for an explanation, and it transpires that the Libyan leader, pissed off by the failure of his cavalcade to arrive on time, set out to walk into town from Lagos Airport.

'How far did he get?' I enquire.

'Oh,' my friend replies, 'only a couple of hundred yards – he had three hundred heavily armed bodyguards with him.'

I push the slick nodule, and, slumbering, dream of the Guide of the First of September Great Revolution of the Socialist People's Libyan Arab Jamahiriya, his green robes flapping in the fume-laden convections as he trudges resolutely off on his walk from Tripoli to Lagos, a walk that sucks the very Sahara from the bedrock and sends it, a plume of sand, twisting into the sky . . .

. . . and wake to hear the tail end of the safety announcements, and the only address that truly matters, the one to the crew: 'Doors to automatic and cross check.' We're off, the jumbo tromping leadenly around the precincts of the terminal, then picking up speed and trumpeting into the sky. Sequestered in the howdah sits a mahout in headphones, a sturdy unexcitable fellow: Saint-Exupéry with a semi in Staines.

I have no business here in business class. The man in the pod next to me – we form a copula, anonymous lovers spent by mercantile *soixante-neuf* – has a Ken Follett paperback tented on his thigh, while a VDU screen obscures his fleshy face. He changed into tan chinos before takeoff and asked the stewardess for a Diet Sprite that she was unable to provide. Hell, this is still England, after all.

When the seatbelt light is extinguished I rise and amble to a gap where I can do some stretching. First, hand on a seatback, I hold one leg up against the oppos-ing buttock, like an ageing Antinous; then, arms braced against a bulkhead and the other leg extended, I push the plane westwards. My late friend Jason Schone taught me these simple exercises, ways of warding off stiffness, which even at the age of forty-two I knew nothing of.

That was on my first radial walk, out from the London epicentre. I picked Jason up at Pickett's Lock, near Edmonton, and headed on with him, up into Epping Forest. It was a hot after-noon in early July 2003, and we talked and walked. I'd known Jason for four years, having met him the first day I'd cleaned up from drugs. He was on the same long walk back to some semblance of sanity – but he kept lagging behind, straying into methadone swamps and dopey thick-ets. His health was already

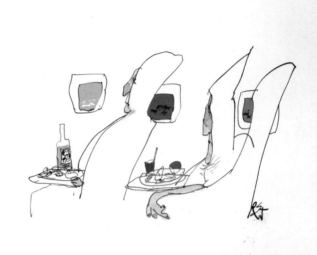

poor – hepatitis, diabetes – he really needed to keep up. On that glorious, dappled afternoon we were in step and he told me much about his life. Then, like Nick Papadimitriou, Jason was abandoned – the first stage of a rocket I'd employed to exit the surly gravity of the conurbation. I left him at Epping Tube Station, and while I blasted on into the outer space of Essex, he fell back, end over end, and splashed down into the oceanic city.

I remember looking back at Jason standing on the platform, the PA announce-ments of westbound trains crackling through the gloaming. The spark of electricity and the hum of the rails. I saw him a few times after that – but only a few. He died, trekking in Nepal two years later, and was cremated in a hill village. Why drag his body back to London? He was never especially happy here. Places, I often feel, choose people, not the other way round. Tourism is a search for a place that will embrace you; sex tourism a dreadfully wrongheaded transference.

In truth, I get bored in Manhattan. It's the late spring of 1992, and I'm sitting in an oh-so-hip loft apartment off Spring Street, my head tilted up at an odd angle, 41 watching through a transom as the rain falls: streams of water as thick and iron-black and oblique as the fire escapes hanging off the fronts of the buildings across the way. Sitting there, stoned on weed, and feeling the whole dead weight of my dead mother's misery and frustration, feeling it as if I'm wearing hand-me-down lead boots and a copper helmet. Suited in my mother's claustrophobia, breathing her stale anxiety, I'm diving down, deep beneath New York, and it's pressuring me, these millions of tons of masonry, of steel, of iron and glass. It's on my back, this Platonic ideal of a city, which always strikes me as a single, undifferentiated block, from which individual skyscrapers have been carved out.

Flash forward to Now + four days. Another friend, the novelist Zoë Heller, who, after flying back and forth over the Atlantic for some years, roosted in Manhattan in 1994, and now has an American husband and children, expostulates 'Dull as ditchwater!' She is in her loft apartment, hard by the Holland Tunnel, but referring to the London skyline.

I beg to differ, both now and then. Caroming in from JFK, over the Queensboro Bridge, that great berm of mud-brown housing – public projects and private apartments – that Robert Moses bulldozed into being from 23rd Street to the Brooklyn Bridge, has always struck me as being quite as dull as ditchwater. Looking as it does, as if all the interwar, redbrick housing estates that London has to offer, have been cemented together and raised up into a mighty, tedious baffler. The chrome watchtowers and steely spires of Midtown are mere pinpricks set beside this! And besides, when I'm in Midtown I feel even *deeper* down, and the rain falls from an even *greater* height. In London the rain is, at worst, only one or two storeys high, but there . . .

I remember that afternoon in SoHo because it was on my first, conscious trip to New York; and even an experienced apathete such as myself – the shirker of the Taj Mahal, the dodger of the Alhambra – was still struck by how inappropriate this seemed. Having body-swerved the city in the late 1970s and throughout the 1980s, when its colonisation by Brits posh and penurious alike made the notion of going there myself altogether *too much*.

There was this justification and there was also my mother's lock on New York, her proprietorship. When you're small your parents loom large, and their places must, congruently, be smallish. All of New York was Mother's fiefdom – she its absentee landlord, a *rentier* living off the glamorous capital she'd acquired there in the 1940s and 1950s. She went every year, sometimes twice. She had a lover there and therefore New York, far from being the city that never slept, was the city where my sexagenarian mother went to sleep. Perhaps retaining it, thus, unrealised save for episodes of *Kojak* and the car chase sequence in *The French Connection*, was a way of not having to visualise her *at it*?

But the Brits in New York, with their gee-whizz and their oh-my-gosh gush, and their wide-eyed approbation of all things big, expansive and American. I could do without it – and them. Without even troubling to go there I knew that I wouldn't share their enthusiasm. In part, this had to be political: the Brits who went to New York at that time were in flight from what they viewed as a failed state, a bankrupt rust bucket that had taken on IMF pilots. They brought back cocaine, chewing gum and Monetarism; the latter an economic doctrine of such tautologous vacuity that it reduced the mental states of an entire class of people to a series of lower case letters (where 'i' = inflationary wage claims).

Yet also it was my own childhood experience. When my father took a sabbatical at Cornell in the mid-1960s, I had a year at grade school in Ithaca, upstate New York. This was an era, when, to a short-trousered, bat-eared boy from un-centrally heated England, the States were pure futurism: multiplex cinemas, automatic cars, electric carving knives, Orange Julius spearing the moment with his pitchfork. This early exposure to America did for it as a new-found-land, made it part of the furniture of my psyche, coextensive with Aertex shirts and the smell of brake blocks on new bicycles bought at Kilburn High Road. So, having pledged allegiance to the flag for a year, over the subsequent twenty-five I ran it down the flagpole. No one saluted.

Then, in 1988, Mother died, at the Royal Ear Hospital in London, and perversely, as the World Spirit of urbanity sped eastwards to merge with her dispersing and troubled psyche, so I found myself, after a further half-decade, at last able to head west. To that loft apartment in SoHo; to New York, where on the previous day I had ascended to the 107th floor observation deck of the South Tower of the World Trade Center. There I had looked north to see the grey verge of Manhattan, lying between the dull waters of the Hudson and the East ditches.

Throughout the remainder of the 1990s and into the new millennium, I had continued to visit New York; but these were the exact opposite of the radial walks that now score my presence, deeper and deeper into the matter of London. These were the travelling equivalent of skipping stones, with me a flat pebble, flipped out of the sky over Long Island, bouncing once in New York, then shooting off at a crazy angle to dip down in Boston, then Chicago, then Minneapolis, and so on, across America. Touching the meniscus of each city long enough to read from a few pages of one of my books, scrawl a few dedications, spout a few press interviews and get drunk.

43

I found myself in Boston on 20 May 1993, 'Cheers Day'. As the last episode of the folksy barroom sitcom aired, and companionable crowds celebrated, I was alone in my hotel room drinking miniatures. Very few people knew my name. This was the shape of my times in the USA: seven-, fourteen- and twenty-one-city book tours, intended to put my product 'on the wall', as the American marketing parlance would have it. There were other trips Stateside to write features, and even some purely to see my half-brother, Nick Adams, who teaches at Vassar College; but mostly, I went there to work.

I would say – and believe it when I did so – that as I came through Customs, and headed straight for the first bar, and ordered a Scotch on the rocks, or a vodka martini, straight up, a great weight would slide from my shoulders: the whole, miserable, class-bound heft of Olde Englande, that rived one man from his brother on the next barstool along. This was bullshit: the truth was that although I might have chatted more readily to Norm or Cliff, it was only because we were all citizens of the United State of Drunkenness.

Perhaps the most horrifying touring experience of all – and there were many, believe me – was when, staggering through Logan Airport, I found myself ordering a matitudinal beer inside an entire mock-up of the interior of *Cheers*, complete with waxworks of Norm and Cliff propped to the right and the left of me.

And New York, what was that? A city I fled into and then escaped from. A city in which even the grid pattern wasn't simple enough for me, for I wanted to go from Elaine's, uptown, to drink at Marylou's down in the Village, and then to my restless bed in the grim enclosure of the Gramercy Park Hotel, ridden on a monorail of cocaine. The Strand Bookstore, on Broadway, south of Union Square, lured me in with its '22 miles of second-hand books'; yet I couldn't have walked a tenth of these shelves. I was strung out, suffering a comedown from drug America, appalled by gimcrack light fitments, flimsy electric plugs, rusty water tanks and toilet stalls as flimsily protective of my modesty as matchbooks – the very quiddity of the place both massively irked me and was painfully familiar. I expected at any second to turn a corner and find myself back in the Gray's Inn Road.

When my future wife came with me for a weekend to Manhattan in 1996 she, too, was underwhelmed. At a ritzy party, thrown for the actor Al Pacino on the Upper East Side, movie star guests and toney journalists stood about. There was no sign of the Big Pastrami, until, after a couple of hours, we were approached by a gofer:

'Al will see you now,' he said, gesturing towards an inner sanctum.

'But we don't want to see him!' we both expostulated; and this confirmed us in our shared obtuseness, our defiant unwillingness to be impressed – let alone assimilated. We didn't want to see Al, we didn't want to enter any inner revolve and be slowly turned to face another actor, one who didn't even have a script.

A year or so later, walking on Hallowe'en up from the Village to Midtown, carrying our infant son, we were checked by reveller after reveller, their vampiric make-up bleeding under the streetlights. 'Is that baby, like, real?' they queried. To which I might just as happily have replied: 'Is your city?' For I had done everything I could to reduce it to the status of a set, upon which I adopted my own hammy poses.

I have set little of my fiction in New York: the closing scene of my first novel took place in the Oyster Bar at Grand Central (I've always felt at home in an oyster); a story, 'Caring, Sharing', features neurotic, kidult New Yorkers, cared for by genetically engineered giants; and then my third novel, *How the Dead Live*, contained some New York scenes, extrapolated from my own mother's verbal accounts of her life in the wartime city.

Forty-nine days after 9/11, I found myself walking through Union Square with my eldest son, then eleven years old. A candle-bearing group of Buddhists were

holding a ceremony to mark the end of the *bardo*, the wandering of the souls that had been expunged from their material bodies by the attacks on the Twin Towers. I thought of my mother, who in the novel is resurrected as Lily Bloom, only to discover that the Tibetan Buddhist cosmology obtains, and she is doomed by her own rancour, forever to repeat the go-round of birth and death and birth again. Not even this: not even the smoky, chthonic pit beyond Vessey Street, or the heart-aching flyers advertising the dead-presumed-missing that fluttered on every hoarding and phone booth, could jerk me out of it and make me where I was. In Manhattan I walked abroad in my mother's caul.

When, on my next trip to New York, I was stopped at JFK and almost deported, the Deputy Head of Immigration said to me: 'I don't care if you *choose* to live in London. I don't even mind if you travel on a British passport – when you're *abroad* – but when you come here, to the United States of America, *you are an American!*' I was carried away by the sheer joy of being picked for the team – any team – at last. Me, the clumsy kid with the fat thighs! Yet the feeling of warm inclusion soon faded. Never did I feel less American than when I officially became one. And let's remember: US citizenship has a religious quality; it can be renounced purely verbally, just as all it takes to become a Muslim is a speech act.

We half-breeds, we fish-fowl chimeras, we're always defining ourselves both by what we are not and what we are (not). Hell, let's not get carried away by this, but in mid-Atlantic, as the stewardess awakens me from my slumber to present me with the TV dinner that accompanies this teleological show – shrimp cocktail, stir-fried chicken, the obligatory aerated dessert, a chock of Stilton cheese, Green & Black's miniature chocolate bar, bubbly mineral water – it all impinges anew: the sense I have of being both stateless and, at one and the same time, the very model citizen of a nine-thousand-mile-long nation, that stretches from Honolulu to Hull.

46      If I were myself to be so elongated, and become Blakean time-goo pulled from

blocky, reified time, no doubt I would sense the presence of myself, in another plane – a Boeing 757 this time – coming back the other way, pushing towards Heathrow. In it, in an identical pod, I'm curled up, writing this essay. The walk done, now it is being described. I'm eating the beef bourguignon, the wincey potatoes and dwarf carrots, while dabbling with the obligatory, aerated dessert, and still I cannot forbear from following the progress of *The Ant Bully*, or losing myself in the photographs of Oxford that suborn the utility of the plane's bulkheads.

# Walk Two: Suburban New York

Down the crystal hill we toboggan, leaping over cols and schussing into arêtes of the air, then the wardrobe clunk of the plane landing and its trundle into JFK. I'm off first and striding along corridors with floors speckled pale blue, grey and green: the Pointillism of the institutional. New countries are, first and foremost, new colour schemes. The ideal immigrant is a wannabe interior decorator. No queue at Immigration, because I've swapped one passport for the other. Nevertheless, I've come here, to the United States of America, and I am as alien as if I'd pulled up to the stand in a flying saucer, because while every single person in this terminal is going to roll out of it tonight, I'm intent on striding.

This has always been the most worrying part of the walk to New York, the egress from JFK. All the maps are worse than useless. They show expressways and beltways and parkways – but indicate no pedestrian rights of way. I cannot tell, from the map, if roads are elevated or sunk in the ground. The intersections between service roads and throughways may be equipped with sidewalks, or only cold, hard shoulders. Like I said, I had heard of one man who'd walked out of JFK, I even know him, but I couldn't do anything as sensible as ask him how he did it. No, with a very British lack of preparedness – like Robert Falcon Scott, eschewing the huskies – I relish this terra incognita, this genuinely newfound land.

Striding outside the terminal for a cigarette, I pace, puffing, up and down the confines of the sidewalk. Darkness has fallen, it's 9.00 p.m., and beyond this oasis, planted with light palms by the overhead lighting, the concrete bled of the airport is all around. I can see cabs, the lifts up to the Skytrain, private cars picking up and dropping off, but no conceivable way of exiting the terminal except along the roadway itself.

Back inside I approach the Ground Transportation desk, just for the hell of it: this is staffed by Elizabeth and Keisha, the former heavyset and dour, the latter young and enthusiastic. Keisha is, it transpires, a Trinidadian-American. Elizabeth couldn't be less interested in my need to walk out of JFK, but Keisha — once I've explained how I've already walked from my London home to Heathrow – gets it:

'Oh, I see!' she exclaims, 'It's, like, a quest.'

No, no, it *is* a quest – there's no likeness implied. It's a quest for identity, and a search to find that urgent commingling of blood and soil. But no matter what enthusiasm she may possess, Keisha still has no idea of how to walk out of JFK. It's left to me to hitch up my nylon rucksack, pull down my tweed cap, and step off the kerb into the night. It's warm in this, the Country of the Climate Change Deniers, and the man wearing a cashmere pullover under a cagoule is a poltroon. Within yards of the terminal I'm sweating – while striding purposefully along the hard shoulder, my own synthetic one swishing against the crash barrier.

Luckily, the airport is shutting down for the night, so traffic passes me in little fits and hissing spurts. That I'm dressed in black is providential; even so, every second I expect a police siren to squawk and blades of blue light to slash through the orangey morass. In the mid-distance I can see the Kennedy Expressway, paring away towards the Nassau. How am I going to avoid being sucked into this? Will there be a slip road out of here? A hundred metres, two hundred . . . five hundred . . . and there it is! A single-lane chute up and away from this trackless waste of tarmac. At the top there's a homely stop sign, then it falls back down again to join another highway, but at least here there's a verge.

Plodding along this, still sweaty and fearful, I see a taxi lot over on the far side. Where there's a taxi lot, I figure, there has to be a way out of the airport at street level. Should I risk crossing six lanes and two crash barriers to reach it? Or should I keep on keeping on? After another 500 metres and no sign of a way forward, I decide on the traverse, and start off, only to beat a retreat when a swarm of enemy chariots bears down on me.

At last, I see a second slip road. It leads me to the right, loops under the overpass. I work my way between some cargo hangars – then suddenly: here I am, strolling across the bridge over the Belt Parkway and on to 150th Street. I'm no longer in terra nullis, I'm in South Ozone Park, NY. A gas station looms up ahead and it looks like the cosiest, most *gemütlich* thing I've seen in all my born days. There's a thicket of Stars and Stripes planted by the doors.

Inside there's a charming Asian clerk with band aids on the fingers of one hand and a rubber glove on the other. He's sold out of Poland Spring Water. A black man stands by a rack of Hershey Bars and M&Ms, rubbing at a scratch card with a dime. The front page of the *New York Post* features the 'bimbo summit' of Lindsay Lohan, Britney Spears and Paris Hilton. Clearly, I have stepped on to America.

The Crowne-Plaza Hotel at Baisley Park, Jamaica, has nothing to recommend it save its proximity to the airport – and I like that. I even like my room, which, as is traditional for the unaccompanied male guest, arriving on foot, late in the evening, is right next to the elevator shaft. A restless night ensues; I sleep with the radio on and in between the clunks and whirrs of the elevator, news rolls into me of Danny DeVito, drunk on *The Barbara Walters Show*; the continuing investigation into the shooting by cops of an unarmed black man, Sean Bell, on his stag night in nearby Queens. Further off, 3,500 US troops are being moved to Baghdad from the surrounding provinces, while the Iraq Study Group's report is due within the week. Rumsfeld has taken the fall for all of the Administration, which is being worried in the bloodied jaws of Baghdad.

In the middle of the night I stir and – purely because I can – smoke a cigarette. It's as acridly unpleasant as a chemical incident. As I gargle the toxic gunk, the rolling news throws up on my gritty consciousness this: a story of a killer whale at San Diego Sea World that has taken its trainer in its jaws and worried him, as a terrier might an invasive rat. 'I don't see why he would do that . . .' says a bemused spokesman. Sunni insurgents – killer whales; as we say in London: 'same difference'.

I wake to the weather forecast for *boulevardiers*: a spruce lady in red, in front of the eighty-eight-foot-high spruce outside the Rockefeller Center, which is topped with a Swarovski star. By mid-afternoon, she tells us, the high in Central Park will be 70 degrees, the warmest November day since 1991, and the second warmest ever recorded. I needn't have brought the pullover, or my tombstone of a book, either, *The Power Broker: Robert Moses and the Fall of New York* by Robert A. Caro. My brother sent it to me, in anticipation of my walk. Surely the biography of Moses – the key figure in city planning and governance for nigh on half a century – will be enough to anchor me in the city? After all, Baisley Pond Park, the scrap of Astroturf underlay without the Crowne-Plaza, is a Moses plantation. Isn't this one of the frame of referents that I can peg my observations to, as I trudge through East New York and Brooklyn?

For this is the worry. I may have escaped from the Empty Quarter of JFK, yet Jamaica, Ozone Park, Woodhaven, Brownsville, these – as Midge Ure would doubtless have sung, if faced by the same predicament – mean nothing to me; in place of London's narrative plenitude I'm faced by the blank slate of New York. Will anything occur to me as I plod along? Will I see anything? Talk to anybody? Or might I be thrown back into my own wildly prosaic psychic hinterland, and find myself besieged there, fending off a couplet from a 1970s pop song? 'Everyone's a winner, baby . . .'

Unfortunately, after only a chapter or two it became clear to me that Caro couldn't supply the goods. Not his fault but mine entirely. You cannot implant a lifetime of memories and impressions with a little light reading; you cannot familiarise yourself with a city through the career of its pre-eminent public administrator. Caro's *Power Broker* would be an anchor all right, dragging the rucksack down between my shoulder blades, threatening to yank me on to my back. Gregor Samsa in a black cagoule. Grim.

As to my route, for some reason my brother has pushed the idea that I must head up through Jamaica, then Queens, then over the Queensboro Bridge and on to 58th Street in Manhattan. But I've resisted this, preferring to head west through Brooklyn. I'm staying in the Lower East Side, so why would I want to walk sixty blocks downtown? Besides, I fancy seeing Crown Heights. It seems appropriate, given my healing mission, to pass by the bunker of 'The Rebbe', at 770 Eastern Parkway. Although he died in 1996, Menachem Mendel Schneerson's Lubavitcher sect still dominates the neighbourhood. And it was a car in The Rebbe's motorcade that ran over and killed a black kid in 1991, sparking the subsequent riots. Despite the kicking the Hassidim got, many still revere The Rebbe as the 'moschiach', or messiah.

From the psychogeographic perspective The Rebbe is an interesting case. The back end of his life was spent entirely in Crown Heights, Brooklyn. Latterly, he even refused to leave the Lubavitcher HQ, and after a stroke a 'mini-hospital' was constructed inside the building. From this cloistral gaff, The Rebbe distributed a vast number of carcinogenic fatwas, helping to harden the arteries of US policy in the Middle East. My personal feeling is that he should've got out more.

Another friend, the novelist Rick Moody, who lives at Prospect Heights, has supplied a rough outline of the Brooklyn route, and although he's not a great walker his comments – which include distances, landmarks and fragments of local history – betray a surprisingly intimate awareness of the arrangement of urban parts. Rick, it appears, is someone who knows *where he is*.

First, breakfast. Muesli, juice, fruit, coffee, half-fat milk, more coffee. I'm sluggish in the face of so much carefully arranged carbohydrate. I go to spoon what I assume to be blueberries on to my muesli, only to discover that they're chocolate drops. I'm galvanising my bowels in the bowels of the Crowne-Plaza, surrounded by ornate mirrors, a tiled floor, blown-up photographs of iconic figures – skirty Marilyn, boxy Muhammad-to-be – and a silvery prop plane flying over the Empire State Building.

My father would often say things such as 'Have you got your little sacheverel?' A term for a rucksack that's so recondite I can't find it in the *OED*. He also referred to jackets as 'jerkins', and shoes as 'dancing pumps'. He rambled hither and thither in flannel trousers lashed with a thin leather belt, and from time to time ungirded himself to rearrange the distempered elephant's ears of his flannel underwear. I think of him, forever adrift between the wars, as I pack up in my room, check out, and head back to the lobby to meet my new companion for the first leg of the New York walk.

He's wearing a dark grey suit, a light blue shirt and a darker blue tie. The creases on his longish legs are immaculate, and on his feet are brown Timberlands. He carries a canvas book bag slung over one shoulder, which I later learn contains dress shoes, for he's on his way to a memorial service for one of his former colleagues, Gerald Boyd, who until two years previously was the Managing Editor of the *New York Times*, and who has died of lung cancer, aged fifty-six.

Boyd, perhaps the most senior African-American journalist in the States, took the fall over the case of Jayson Blair, a young protégé of his – also black – who, it transpired, was making up as much copy as he was reporting. For some racists this was all the news that it was fit to print concerning affirmative action. This, I feel certain, is the antithesis of my new companion's attitude. And as for his commitment to the *actualité*, even at 9.00 a.m., Charles 'Chip' McGrath, 'Writer-at-Large' for the *New York Times*, has his spiral-bound reporter's pad to the ready. I didn't know exactly what to expect of McGrath – who I've been corresponding with by email, in order to set up this rendezvous – but I've got it roughly right. He's softly spoken, reserved, urbane. With his greying temples, reticent eyes behind oval glasses and uncertain, grizzled mouth, he looks like a *Muppet Show* sock puppet that also happens to be a Yale alumnus. Statler, Waldorf and McGrath.

As it transpires, Chip is indeed a Yale alumnus, class of '68, the same one as the current Leader of the Free World. Later, when we're trudging past the triumphal arch at Grand Army Plaza, he recounts an anecdote about his classmate with the war-making powers. An extremely disturbing anecdote that he urges me not to repeat; and which I won't, having given my word. Chip has what my mother would've called 'built in orphan power': one wants, instinctively, to cuddle him, not betray his confidence.

He reminds me of my brother Nick's circle: patrician, East Coast intellectuals, more English than the English. At Nick's recent wedding (his second, to a fellow historian), there must have been forty-odd people gathered in the reception rooms of his and Laurie's eighteenth-century clapboard house; yet such was the muted burr of their conversation that you could've heard a bluebottle bat against one of the slow-flowing antique windowpanes. I wondered at the time: are these the vulgarians the European Left seek to immolate? Are these 'the Yanks' that are coming?

Chip is to accompany me some of the way into New York, and write the walk up for a piece in the *New York Times*. I'm divided over this: it certainly compromises my plans; it's difficult to see how a stranger – especially one with his own agenda – is going to help me to either achieve ambulatory *sartori*, or any deeper absorption into the urban landscape. On the other hand, I've come here for a number of reasons, and one of them is to try and publicise my latest novel to be published in the USA; a novel that has received a kicking in the review pages of Chip's own newspaper. Not that this is unexpected, although if any single notice can do for a novel in this country it's a bad one in the *New York Times*. If walking with Chip can somehow redress the negative coverage, then this can only be a good thing. In a world in which a new book is published every forty seconds, what else can a journeyman writer do? I am, it occurs to me, exactly like my great-grandfather Isaac, dressed in black and hawking my skills from literary community to literary community.

After some remarks on unsuitable footwear – Chip contends that, as a golfer, he knows what he's doing – we set off. He's brought a snapper with him, a freelance called Casey Kelbaugh, who has a regulation goatee and a mountain bike. Moving through Baisley Pond Park, and then along North Conduit, Casey circles and recircles us, as if herding our odd couplet.

Initially a little shy, Chip and I soon establish mutual acquaintances then plot out the territory between these landmarks. There's this discourse, and there's also my need to get across to him my quest; to have him take seriously the Gestalt – compounded of place, progress and *Weltanschauung* – which informs my every tread through this dun and unprepossessing 'burb. It's a little uneasy, for me, skipping round him and quoting myself: all interviews are dangerous and destabilising, presenting the opportunity to ape one's own ideal, an opening that must be refused.

North Conduit rumbles with trucks, and the sky is yet low and grey. America announces itself to be parched and desiccated: all seems flatter, lower and wider than Europe. A coil of polythene on the sidewalk recalls Laura Palmer's shrink-wrapped corpse in Lynch's *Twin Peaks*. The signs hanging from the spans of fly-overs direct the traffic back towards the airport. My calf muscles tell me that I am walking for the second day, and this bodily mediation of space is far more powerful than any jet engine. Moreover, Jamaica is believably coextensive with Feltham – it has the same feel of the metropolitan periphery, an interzone, underimagined and seldom depicted. So, to me, it feels as if I have continued to bore, like a worm, through the same urban tree ring.

Chip estimates the prices of these detached white clapboard houses at $400,000, and pronounces South Ozone Park to be 'ethnic'. Here are some of the subjects we discuss as we walk: the Chinese Communist regime – Chip believes they've cut a deal with their citizens: things for democracy. Golf, and in particular Chinese golf – according to Chip the regime is building some interesting, ecologically sound courses. The shootings in Jamaica: nobody would wish to prejudice the enquiry into how it was that the NYPD fired thirty-one shots at the stag party leaving the bar, but Chip has a friend on the force who told him that undercover cops working in such places are allowed one alcoholic drink in the course of their duties, so as to avoid arousing suspicion. Chip thinks it conceivable that some of these officers 'may've abused the privilege'.

Meanwhile, we pass by house after home bedecked with decorations. The balustrades and staircases are hung with leafy wreaths twined with red ribbon. The yards are crowded with Yule entities: snowmen, elves, angels and reindeer, all of them twisted out of fibre-optic cabling. On the front stoops of many of these $400,000 grottoes lie puddles of red and white fabric; slack Santas, who, when evening falls, will be inflated by concealed blowers, so as to wobble there, bulbous heralds of the coming bloat-fest. On a normally brusque November evening, illuminated, these Xmas tableaux might seem a little over the top, examples of peasant atavism, lurid *obeah* in Ozone Park, but in daylight, with the temperature twenty degrees higher than average, they are altogether absurd: seasonal solecisms.

By the Aqueduct Race Track we ask an elderly man for directions, and inadvertently voice our ultimate destination. It isn't fair, really, for he's painfully disoriented by the very fact of our enquiry. Walking to New York? With his cap crammed down on his round head and his hound's-tooth check jacket he looks at us, annoyed: it's we who must be in the wrong, for on this scrap of waste ground, the Race Track looming in the mist, he knows where he is.

Conduit Boulevard: in the mid-distance fifteen-storey project blocks loom over

The labels on the image read:

GLENMORE AVENUE
PRESBYTERIAN CHURCH

SUN Worship 11AM.
Apocalipsis Pentecostal Church
Sun 8 AM. Mon Tues 8 PM
Zion Tabernacle Deliverance Ministry
Sun 1PM Wed 8PM
Full Gospel Tabernacle of Faith & Deliverance
Sun 6PM Fri 7:00 PM
ENY SDA CHURCH
SAT 9AM TH 7:30PM

CHRIST APOSTOLIC CHURCH
OF GOD MISSION INC.

I AM THE WAY,
THE TRUTH, AND THE LIFE/
NO MAN COMETH. UNTO
THE FATHER. BUT BY ME.

CHRIST
APOSTOLIC
CHURCH OF
GOD MISSION
INC.

five-storey mounds of trash. Yellow excavators root their saw-toothed snouts in this machine-age midden. At the junction with Linden Boulevard stands the Linden Motor Inn, a beige, concrete shape that resembles the superstructure of a ship that has been buried in the verge. Even from the far side of six lanes and a broad median strip, I can make out two figures in baseball caps, rooting in a bush beside the motel. They are searching, I presume, for their discarded stash. When we close in on the Linden, I see a sign threatening 'Jacuzzi'.

The cloud has burnt off, and it does, indeed, promise to be a fine spring day in November. I'm a little footsore, and to be frank, verging on sadness. People always say that you can't walk in American cities – implying that the very sidewalks curl up in front of your feet, or that the traffic mows you down. But that isn't it: no one walks through East New York, I'm forced to conclude, because it's so fucking dull. Mile on mile of tract houses and apartment blocks, with only plastic Santas to break the monotony. Popeye's Chicken and Biscuits, offering 'New Naked Chicken Strips, Only 1 Carb per Strip', constitutes a visual feast. Yesterday's stroll beside the Thames, romp through Richmond Park and meditative progress beside the River Crane now looks in my mind's eye like a Watteau, complete with lavender flounces, airborne cherubs and diaphanous, trailing greenery. These memories are paintings hung on the leafless branches of fume-smoked trees.

At last, we swing off the thoroughfare and along Glenmore Avenue. This has a more human scale, even if the humans are obese and surly with poverty. Ragtag people are dumped on benches outside the Brooklyn Adult Care Center at 2830 Pitkin Avenue. Brooklyn has been described as the 'city of a thousand churches', and here they all are: the Apocalipsis Pentecostal Church; the Zion Tabernacle of Deliverance Ministry; St Lydia's Episcopal Church; Christ the Rock Bible Institute; the Universal Temple. They vary wildly in style, from storefront, cinder-block God shops, to shingled Carpenter Gothic, to nineteenth-century banking blockhouses. One is an old synagogue, winnowed out by Christ, another a hefty, Greek Orthodox encampment complete with genetically modified, square-onion domes.

Glenmore Avenue is two arrow-straight miles of churches, frame houses, low-rise apartments. Nowhere in New York – the natives now say, not without a trace of regret – is truly dangerous any more, but this area is one of the poorest. Every twentieth dwelling is a condemned rat's nest, complete with municipal orders pasted to the boarded-up doors and filthy underpants espaliered on the railings.

Ah, the Blighted States of poverty. Survey after survey tells us that the American poor are oddly optimistic about their lot, remaining convinced that even though they may be standing in the welfare line, those armies of global, capitalist salvation are going to sweep down and enlist them. But I don't get that vibe. I think the surveys are filled in by those who self-select for co-option. East New York reeks – albeit in a subdued way – of desperation, of a populace who can never attain that shiny repose, or dream the American Dream. For them there is only the rock, the apocalypse, the End of Days – a chasm full of brimstone, into which are hurled broken white goods.

Clearly, Chip, Casey and I do not belong here, but we attract little attention; there are few people on the streets mid-morning, midweek. Only once, as we near the projects at the end of the avenue, is there a frisson of old New York, the New York of discarded crack vials crunched underfoot and violent, illiterate men with writing on their trousers.

An SUV slows to a crawl along the kerb beside us, its tinted windows pulsing with the confinement of an insistent beat. One of them reels down to reveal four African-American faces giving us the once-over. It reels back up again, and the

SUV moves off, only to circle the block and come level with us once more. 'We're being dicked,' I observe to Chip, 'people are wondering what we're doing on their turf.' Chip seems blithe about this – or perhaps he's preoccupied by something else. I suspect his loafers may be beginning to chafe.

Personally, I would relish the opportunity to engage the gun crew in a discussion of urban territoriality as it relates to topography; this would be the sort of rambling conversation – at once deeply patrician, yet prescriptively egalitarian – that I remember my father having with holidaying coal miners, when we walked from Taunton to Lyme Regis. A divorced father and sulky son walking tour, back in the sunny uplands of the early 1970s.

East New York ends in the metallic gnashing of elevated railway tracks, freight and scrap yards. We stumble past a shut library, my bladder a painfully inflated balloon rammed in my crotch. We turn up Rockaway Avenue and I duck into an abandoned lot to pee. Then we're in Eastern Parkway. A half-mile on and there it is: the ethnic interface I've been waiting for. A Hassidim in a blue sweatshirt with 'KITCHEN EXPO' written across its shoulders, stands chatting to a heavyset black man. Beyond them looms the Holy House of Prayer for All People (semicircular transverse arch, attached half-columns with foliated capitals, this recessed in red brick and strongly reminiscent of the Twickenham Green Baptist Church).

The Parkway rises towards affluence, and we labour up one of the two flanking median strips, past Ralph Avenue and the Trinity Methodist Church. The buildings are putting on weight, becoming solider and more self-assured. We gain Utica Avenue, and this is a proper city junction. There are people on the streets hurrying, with the kind of pecuniary and sumptuary motives that would gratify Adam Smith – or even Milton Friedman. From the entrance to the subway there comes a great meaty, oily, burnt-dust afflatus; down there, New York is moving its bowels, peristaltically pushing its populace through snaking colons and sooty back passages.

Here in the Parc Tower is Wishco Manor, Catering Kosher. Or here, between wars, it once was; for the neon letters are bleary with the years, and above them Washington Mutual reigns, while alongside them there's the indefatigable strength of Popeye with his chicken and biscuits. The *frummers* flap about the place in their ghetto get-ups. Their women – condemned by observance to eternal frumpiness – are less in evidence, and the only school kids I see are boys with skullcaps and spaniel locks, loitering on the steps of a *cheder*.

I poke through the paperbacks for sale on a stall. *Survivor: Outwit, Outplay, Outlast . . . Thailand*; Danielle Steel's *Second Chance*, Frank McCourt's mawkish demi-memoir *'Tis* . . . and a couple of novels by people I know in London.

It's faintly preposterous finding these here; as if they were intimate possessions mysteriously transported across the Atlantic. Indeed, I happen to know that these particular titles have sold in small enough numbers for them to be like the personal effects of their creators. Perhaps this is all contemporary literature is, the staging of an emotional yard sale for strangers on Utica Avenue?

I like to think that, were I without Chip and Casey, I would engage some of the *frummers* in sage politico-religious discourse; encourage them towards a *midrash* that would enlighten us all as to the Divine Ingathering and the Clash of Civilisations. But, just as with the gun crew, I'm deluding myself. Far from being elevated by Crown Heights, I can feel my mood dipping. Far from feeling the walk to New York as an achievement, I'm beginning to think this is just another slog away from commitment and engagement, and towards empty-headedness. The Hassidim, it occurs to me, so mirror – with their literalism and their theocratic zeal

– that which they revile; that they are like Calibans in homburgs, checking their appearance in the humungous pier glass of a glassy office block, only to become enraged by the brown face staring back at them: another Semite who's sought asylum on Prospero's isle.

Besides, why are Chip and Casey still with me? Is it something I've said or done? Chip was only meant to walk for an hour or so, but he's been dogging me for four now. It's 1.15, time for lunch, and still he lopes along with his book bag full of dress shoes, and his urbane conversation that so keeps urbanity at bay. The truth is, we agreed a few miles back that he'd gone over the tipping point, and the seesaw of the walk was now impelling him down towards Manhattan. Hell, he might as well come the whole way, and be the third man to have walked in from JFK. It'll be something to tell his womenfolk, should they need a sedative.

Past the Philadelphian Sabbath Cathedral, once a beautiful 1920s movie theatre, now decorticated by religion so that only the Art Deco husk remains. Then, for the purposes of enthusing Chip, as we reach the Brooklyn Museum and can see, in the notch of Washington Avenue, the towers of Midtown piercing the lunchtime smog, I go into a riff, imagining the skirling skein of a mournful clarinet slung out from the city to lasso me with its plaintiff notes: 'Wawawawaaaawawawawaaawawawawawawaaaaaaaaaaaa . . .! *Rhapsody in Blue*, yes, Gershwin's jazzy hymn to holy New York. What could be a better tocsin to awaken a footsore slogger, who's parted the Atlantic with his Gore-Tex boots, to the delights of this Canaan?

But unfortunately I've long since traduced this tune. Its synaesthetic horrors were confirmed for me by a bad acid trip in Oxford, in 1979, when, having pushed the button of a wickedly red microdot into my still-plastic psyche, I mistakenly chucked a '78 of it on to the turntable, only to hallucinate a Hades, populated by galvanised skeletons, banging out the 'diddleumdumdumdiddleumdumdumdiddleumdumdum!' on the ribs of their fellows. Gross, it tipped me into a colloidal cesspit, where every thought or action whipped up thick waves of agonising nausea. I ended up lying at the bottom of a great, hollow spire, the interior of which was lined with thousands upon thousands of rows of disembodied mouths; all of them wide open, all of them screaming . . . nothing.

In my novel *How the Dead Live* I employed *Rhapsody in Blue* as the metallic death rattle of Lily Bloom, the protagonist based on my own mother. Later, on my return from New York, I looked up the relevant section and was appalled to find this:

'It's a tune – not a rhapsody. A rinky-dink, tin-pan-crash-bang bit of Yid slickery, played out in the trash choked alleys around Times Square and Broadway. The city of my majority swims towards me now – out of the dusty deathly darkness of this suburban room an ocean away. At first I'm relieved to have this effortless ascendancy, rising in a smooth parabola from the coxcomb of Liberty into the clouds over the toe of Manhattan, so that the leggy length of the island rears below me, each neon street switched on by my own awareness.

"Diddleumdumdumdiddleumdumdumdiddleumdumdum!" A set of a certain unreal age, with no distinction between the fabricated and the constructed; between interior and exterior. A musical New York peopled by eternally young songsters clad in sky blue Runyon shmatte. See them dance down the block, pirouette around the corner, leap into the subway, while Top Cat trades gags with Officer Dibble and the Jetsons head home in their flivvers to White Plains.'

Egregious, perhaps, to quote oneself, and contrived to use the future past – an uncomfortable tense at the best of times – in which to do so. But there it is, and it's

not nice. Worse still, the resumption of this familiar Manhattan ennui, of interior-exteriority, is what I felt as I walked through Prospect Park to its highpoint, and failed to find any prospect at all. And this is what I continued to feel as we moved down through Grand Army Plaza, and Chip told me his Bush anecdote, which made the lame duck President seem even more hateful, in a kick-in-the-shins, frat-boy kind of a way. And this is what I felt as we proceeded on down Flatbush Avenue, and then stopped in at the Burrito Bar and Kitchen to eat unleavened satchels full of spicy meat paste to the noise of the Doobie Brothers.

And this is what I felt as, flatulent as the subway itself, I moved off down the scrag-end of Flatbush Avenue, turned into Tillary Street, and at last gained the approach to the Brooklyn Bridge. *Rhapsody in Blue* had grabbed me, all right, and shifted me into a simpler – yet even more savage – past. My mother's idiolect was like an infestation of head lice, irritating my psyche. Her savage putdowns: 'emotionally tight-fisted', 'dull', 'weak'; her delight in the expression 'chagrined'. I recalled the desperate entry in her diaries, describing the final occasion on which she went to her ex-lover's studio apartment on Fulton Street, to retrieve her pitiful little things. Impedimenta she had attempted to place in that interior, in the hope of warding off the dreadful and approaching agoraphobia of death itself.

Standing in the middle of the gargantuan harpsichord that is the Brooklyn Bridge, I looked around at helicopters, launches, cyclists, the stalled traffic and the steady trains on the Manhattan Bridge – yet still I was enfolded in that dreadful interior-exteriority: my mother's clarinet moan and faltering snare drum heartbeat, resounding across the ocean. She had died twenty years before, in the Royal Ear Hospital; yet only now did it feel as if I were truly listening. And because we had to – being within a few blocks of the pit – Chip and I fell to discussing 9/11, for not to do so would've been to leave a gaping, narrative hole. The walk without talk of this would've been like seeing *Jaws*, digitally re-edited so as to omit every reference – verbal or visual – to the shark.

Chip was about to enter the Lincoln Tunnel on a bus when he saw the smoke rise up across the Hudson. The cell phones went down – and his denial went up. He returned home to his New Jersey 'burb, and sat there, like a kid playing truant from school, uncomprehending of what had happened. And still uncomprehending, after many days, despite the dust furring the windscreens of the cars slumped in the commuter bus parking lot. Cars, the drivers of which were never to return.

At the base of one of the columns of the colonnade that runs alongside the municipal building at Centre and Chambers Streets in Manhattan, a Muslim was buckled in prayer on a rush beach mat. His white sneakers were off and neatly arranged next to him, and the grey seat of his trousers was in the air. Next to his lowered head, the stone was stained where discarded gum had been unpicked. Mecca may have been his ultimate objective, but to me it looked as if he were making obeisance to Manhattan itself.

The day was clouding over, and it impinged on me, looking up at the umpteen storeys of the block – its cut-and-shut architecture, reminiscent of a Loire chateau that has been customised into a stretch limo – that in Manhattan's very elevation lay its decline. Only the gods lease office space on Olympus; yet here, on the twentieth, thirtieth, fortieth floor, a man picks his teeth with a paperclip, a woman adjusts her bra strap. Mars and Venus send out for pastrami on rye.

I was weary – so was Chip. As I suspected, he'd developed a blister. He left us at the first subway station, limping off through the afternoon crowds, his book bag bumping on his shoulder. Casey and I kept on, and the snapper, who'd spent the whole day circling around me on his mountain bike, as if I were visual carrion, now took on the role of my Virgil, leading me into the next circle of urban hell. We paused to examine a fanciful Chinese grotto – dinky greenery water plashing into teensy pools, the whole wreathed in dry-ice vapour, that was for sale on stall. Casey told me that there are forty thousand registered professional photographers in Manhattan. You can make of that what you will.

It was foolish of me to imagine that I could heal anything with my feet; after all this wasn't a demonstration. Besides, I can't stand marches: mass walking seems such a singularly inappropriate way of promoting peace and understanding. We went on the first of the big anti-war marches in London, in the autumn of 2002, and found ourselves trapped on the Embankment behind a claque of Muslim Association of Britain zealots, all of them screaming 'Death to Israel!' Too much death in the air already – we thought, too much hatred. The children were repelled – so were we. We hung on for a while then turned tail and marched back across Waterloo Bridge to Chez Gerard, where we demonstrated our opposition to all conflict by eating steak and escargots.

It was an equally dumb idea to walk to New York. Wending my way through Little Italy, looking at the Christmas decorations strung from those oblique black fire escapes, I was conscious only of the heavy straps of sore muscle, stretched and then bunched at the backs of my calves. I could feel the sweaty pads of my socks scrunching into the toes of my boots. It had worked, though, walking to New York. It had done exactly what I wanted it to do: the Atlantic had been siphoned off, the continental shelf jacked up, and Hayes, Middlesex, had been rammed unceremoniously into South Ozone Park.

That I had walked, continuously, from Stockwell in south London to Rivington Street in the Lower East Side of Manhattan, could not be denied – for my body told me that this was so; that it had covered some thirty-five miles over the past two days. And the body's awareness is so much more plangent than that of any mere mind. Bodies like mine have been walking distances like these for hundreds – Yea! thousands – of millennia; what can a few score years of powered rolling and whistling flight mean set beside this immemorial trudge?

My hotel stood opposite the Economy Candy Store (since 1937). I said farewell to Casey and entered. Two floors up, in Reception, functionaries in black Mao tunics caressed their keyboards, while behind them a flat-screen monitor displayed an immaculate counterpane being disarranged by invisible hands. When the data-base maiden asked me if I'd had a good trip, I resisted the impulse to tell her I'd walked there from London. I've done this before, in similar circumstances, and the truth is: it gets you nowhere.

Another six storeys up and there it was: the floor-to-ceiling windows faced directly north, over the low rise of Greenwich Village to Midtown. The Chrysler Building and the Empire State, silver and gold urban jewellery, glinted in the late afternoon sun, which, purely to welcome me, had made a last, fleeting appearance. In the bathroom the freestanding sarcophagus of the bathtub sneered at me. I twisted the faucet and water, ridiculously, streamed from a hole in the ceiling. How I loathe hotels, establishments that try to convince you both that domesticity can be hired and that shitting is an 'occasion'.

# Epilogue

Two days later I was upstate. It was breakfast time, and I sat eating croissants with my brother and sister-in-law at their house in Amenia Union. Their new kitten, Tyco, scratched at his twine-coiled post, while through the austere twenty-four-pane windows I looked out over a bend in the road and the desiccated withies of New England's century-old reforestation.

Since the walk to New York had ended, it was as if it had never been. Or rather, when, after a further day of tramping around Manhattan, I gave up and hailed a cab at St Mark's Place to take me uptown, the walk was instantly turned sepia by the smirch of exhaust. It had happened in another era and I was back from the Renaissance. Since then there had been further cabs, and subways and trains and cars, all of them driving me further and further away from whatever point it had been that I was trying to make.

True, I had come to New York, I had done my business, and the following morning I would be flying home again. Yet the existence of the seven-thousand-odd-mile-wide territory that my feet had shaped into being didn't make me, personally, feel any less cut off from the main. In my recollection, the London leg of the walk was a sunny upland, with the riverine city snuggled between wooded hills. By contrast, New York was all dun ground, grey skies and the charcoal strokes of leafless trees. Any sense of the topography was eroded by the human presence:

the weight of their termite heaps, the pyroclastic floes of their automobiles, the nematode boring of their subsurface trains. In Oedipal terms this was all vastly unfair: hadn't it been Mother who mopped my fevered brow, made of illness a cosy discourse, fed me, watered me? While Dad, what did he do save take me for the occasional long walk?

Talking to my brother, I asked why exactly it was that he'd assumed I'd be walking from JFK through Queens to Manhattan.

'Oh, because Mother grew up there, of course. I thought you realised.'

'She always told me she grew up on Long Island, although, come to think of it, I never asked her where.'

Nick explained this discrepancy by pointing out that a Jewish girl, growing up in interwar Queens, but already with one foot on the first rung of the ladder up and out, might well choose to gloss her origins thus. To me, who had reached my majority in the north London suburbs, such posturing still seemed counterintuitive. All my own childhood I had wanted to *get in* there, if necessary to entomb myself in Charing Cross itself. Surely to be urban was always to be cool? Surely it was better to be within the Five Boroughs – and hence a bone fide Noo Yawker – than out in the sticks. Nick said: not so.

Then he admitted that while he knew Mother had grown up in Kew Gardens, near Forest Hills, he didn't know precisely where – he'd certainly never visited the apartment or house. And while I had felt certain, on reviewing this omission in my own geography, that her failure to tell me was a product of the fact that we were never in New York together, Nick said that she hadn't volunteered this information to him either.

There it was, the reason why the walk had seemed so limp, so inconclusive. I had missed my ambulatory connection, why, within an hour of leaving the Crowne-Plaza at Baisley Pond Park, I could've been standing outside my mother's natal home; if, that is, I had known its location.

It was then that my brother switched into one of his most efficient modes: that of professional researcher. Within minutes he had established which directory might furnish me with the address, and where it could be found. A few minutes more and he'd found out which train I should catch back into the city. A scant half-hour later, I was waving goodbye to him as the Metro-North train pulled out of Brewster. Like the Trinidadian girl at JFK, my brother understood the notion of a quest perfectly well.

Some time later, after the train had clanked out of White Plains, and before it had rattled into Harlem at 125th Street, I saw another hunk of cut-and-shut architecture to the side of the tracks near Bronxville. The exposed black beams and white plaster of a Tudor house, raised up on a huge, redbrick plinth. Like all Tudorbethan, it seemed to imply that the Henrician dynasty had endured for nigh on half a millennium; all of us waiting for an heir, while the King himself grew fatter and fatter. But, really, the apartment block was another harbinger.

Caught up in my quest for Mother, memories of her came unbidden: Flat Rock outside Ithaca, wax lips, the automatic Rambler car, her doodles – not unlike the Jetsons' animations   her psychotropic migraines, the distempered rubber of her punitive girdles – incontinent memories of mother, pissing down from the silvery skies over New York.

In the Genealogy Section at the New York Public Library, the librarian referred me to the cabinet where I could find the microfiche of *Polk's Directory* for 1931. This, I hoped, would list my grandfather's residence in Kew Gardens. In a sense, I was way too late already. There was nothing to discuss – and no one to discuss it with. Also, like other middle-aged amateur genealogists, myopia was smearing my eyes. I had to borrow a magnifying glass off a lady, and even then the print appeared horribly tiny and dense. I fiddled to manifest my destiny, with knobs and cranks and lenses. Then, there it was – or they were: two Jack Rosenblooms that could, plausibly, be him. Two addresses in Kew Gardens that might be his: one at Talbot Place, the other directly on the Union Turnpike.

Back in 42nd Street I found it impossible to take a cab. I flexed my arm experimentally – but it wouldn't rise. I was, I realised, finally oriented in New York. I had located myself more completely in the city in the past four days than I had in the preceding fourteen years. I took the uptown local to 51st Street, walked through the connecting corridors to Lexington and 3rd, then took the E train out to Queens. Sitting in the jolting carriage, looking at the two Hispanic guys, their auditory canals connected directly to one another's by the wires of an iPod, it dawned on me that I too was now connected. At last, I had taken up my mother's New York mantle.

I had read up on Kew Gardens before I left my brother's house. I knew it was an interwar suburb, consciously named by its developers, at the turn of the twentieth century, after the famous botanical gardens in London. I also knew to expect 'English' and 'neo-Tudor'-styled houses, interspersed with apartment blocks. I also knew that, like many an outer London suburb, Kew Gardens had first burgeoned because of the train that ran out from the city to the cemetery. Yet what nothing could've prepared me for was the *feel* of the place.

The prosperous, detached houses; the small, unitary shopping parades; the homely, brick apartment blocks; the Saturday afternoon drivers and pedestrians – purposive, yet not rushed. This was not the flitting déjà vu that Tarkovsky captures in his killing jar of a lens, this was not something I had ever seen before – or had even been tricked by synaptic glitch into *believing* I had seen before – no, Kew Gardens was somewhere I *knew*.

I knew the Kew Gardens Cinema, the Maple Grove Cemetery and the Leah B. Weinberg Early Childhood Center. I re-encountered the childlike simplicity of Public School 99, with its cheerful motto 'Two Buildings, One Heart', and, most especially, I recognised 8300 Talbot Place, a four-square, nine-storey apartment block, the honeyed brickwork of which gave off palpable waves of comfortable familiarity in a way that was – as the Germans might say – distinctly *unheimlich*.

I could picture my grandfather up there only too well: his fleshy nose, his slick vest, his money clip with the mother-of-pearl Indian head. I could picture my pretty grandmother as well, painting her laboured still lives of hard-working flowers. I could picture my uncle, in knickerbockers, and my mother, her curly hair in bunches. I could smell the food and dust of the rooms; I could hear the acrimony of their arguments.

Why? It dogged me as I walked back to the subway. Why had my mother omitted to mention, at any point in my childhood, that the north London suburb we lived in was an exact simulacrum of the New York neighbourhood she herself had grown up in? That Kew Gardens and East Finchley were located on the same Möbius strip, a ring of dendro-urbanity that, though it may have grown, twisting through time and space, nonetheless left our senses of place unavoidably on the *same side*.

Presumably because she couldn't stand it: couldn't stand the fact that she had moved and moved and moved again, changing places and jobs and husbands and eventually continents, only to end up somewhere recognisably the same. I couldn't blame her: I couldn't stand it myself. I'd walked all this way, only to discover that I'd never left home at all.

# South Downs Way

I've taken to long-distance walking as a means of dissolving the mechanised matrix which compresses the space-time continuum, and decouples human from physical geography. So this isn't walking for leisure – that would be merely frivolous, or even for exercise – which would be tedious. No, to underscore the seriousness of my project I like a walk which takes me to a meeting or an assignment; that way I can drag other people into my eotechnical world view. 'How was your journey?' they say. 'Not bad,' I reply. 'Take long?' they enquire. 'About ten hours,' I admit. 'I walked here.' My interlocutor goggles at me; if he took ten hours to get here, they're undoubtedly thinking, will the meeting have to go on for twenty? As Emile Durkheim so sagely observed, a society's space-time perceptions are a function of its social rhythm and its territory. So, by walking to the business meeting I have disrupted it just as surely as if I'd appeared stark naked with a peacock's tail fanning out from my buttocks while mouthing Symbolist poetry.

My publishers were holding a sales conference in Eastbourne and I agreed to go along and address the bourgeforce. I decided to entrain from Victoria to Lewes and then walk the South Downs Way the final twenty-two miles. This would be a nostalgic walk, putting myself securely back in my father's world of pipe-smoking, voluminous grey flannel trousers, chalk downland, Harvey's Bitter, Bertie Russell, nudism, the Peace Pledge Union . . . Gah! Christ! I can't breathe in this interwar period . . . I'd better come up for air. Even though I was nominally born in 1961, my father made sure that I too was raised in the interwar period, and we roamed the South Downs a great deal together during my childhood. 'It seemed perfectly natural,' said the minicab driver who took me from Lewes Station to the start of the walk, speaking of his own ambulatory upbringing . . . but I'm getting ahead of myself.

Having consulted maps and timetables I was faced with a dilemma. Should I wait for the branch line train from Lewes to Southease, where I could join the South Downs Way, or should I gain a half-hour by taking a cab there? I dislike cars more than trains – they con their autopilots with the illusion of freedom – but half an hour is significant when you're pushed for walking time. I thought about the options for two long days then called Talking Pages.

Talking Pages had been absorbed into the great telephone-answering gulag known only as '118', so doubtless my call was answered by a Mongolian former yak herder deep in the Altai Mountains. I pictured the call centre wedged like a corrugated spacecraft in some dusty gully. Inside, bandy-legged men in traditional dress slouched about on leather-covered cushions, watching antediluvian videotapes of *Police Five* with Shaw Taylor in order to assimilate the social mores of telephone banking customers in the Potteries. A once-proud nomad doing a passable imitation of a Staffs accent gave me a choice of three minicab companies which served the Lewes area.

Naturally the first two I called turned out to be located in Brighton, despite their Lewes exchange numbers. And, no, they couldn't answer my distinctly local enquiry about the time it takes to drive to Southease. The third company was different. They were located right inside Lewes Station, and, yes, they knew the area intimately. The controller spoke as if every one of his drivers had – like some humanoid nematode – filtered the very earth of Sussex through their bodies. The controller assured me the drive would take mere minutes, so I booked the cab.

The next morning was bright and clear. Sunlight flashed off the braces of orthodontically challenged teenagers who boarded the train at Plumpton on their way to school in Lewes. After detraining, I was so high with anticipation that it wasn't until the cab had gone about two hundred yards in the wrong direction out of Lewes that I pointed it out to the driver: 'I want to be on the east side of the Ouse, at Southease Station.' 'No problem,' he breezed, 'I'll drop you down a track on this side and you can cross the river on the swing bridge.' Then he went on about his childhood, engendering such a warm feeling of mateyness in me that I overtipped the sly fellow.

In fact he'd dropped me outside Rodmell, more than two miles from where I wanted to be. As I puffed along the track, my pipe sending up great clouds of smoke from the Presbyterian tobacco stuffed in it (a blend introduced to Stanley Baldwin in 1923 by the future Moderator of the Church of Scotland), I saw in the mid-distance the little two-carriage train stopping at Southease Station. Now, no matter how hard I walked for the rest of the long day, I would still be lagging behind. The sinuous downs, the soaring Seven Sisters, majestic Beachey Head, all of them suddenly concertinaed into the space between two low-firing synapses in the lazy minicab driver's mind. Machine Matrix 1, Psychogeographers 0. I could hear Durkheim's low and evil laughter in my inner ear. Not a pretty sound.

# On Péages

It's worth considering that the first theoreticians of the railway saw rails and loco-motives as essentially component parts of a single machine. The patents lodged in the early years of the nineteenth century were for rails with projecting 'teeth' which meshed with cog-wheeled engines. Initially it was thought that smooth steel wheels on smooth steel rails simply wouldn't provide the necessary traction, but even when this was proved wrong the French coinage 'chemin de fer' still caused problems for Gallic late adopters: 'Ils y en croient que ces routes sont pavées avec des plaques de fer,' wrote one bemused commentator in 1820, 'mais ce n'est pas cela du tout . . .'

Others first saw the revolutionary transport system as an evolution of existing roadways. In 1802 Richard Lovell Edgeworth published the first proposal to con-struct railways for public transport. He envisaged rails implanted in the highways with heaviest traffic, which would be supplied with cradles on to which existing carriages could be lifted. These would then be drawn on by horsepower, a principle advantage of the system being the reduction in friction. But in a visionary antici-pation of the shape of things to come Edgeworth wrote: 'The chief convenience of this project arises from the mode of receiving and transporting on the rail-ways every carriage now in use without any change in their structure, so that the travel-ler may quit and resume the common road at pleasure.'

Well, delete the word 'pleasure', elide the Frenchman and Edgeworth, and it seems to me we have a pretty accurate description of the *péage* autoroutes which a century later snake across France like blue veins through Roquefort. I know, I know, some will cavil that the highway and the vehicle moving on it don't truly constitute a machine ensemble, because the car is capable of independent motion, but try telling that to a strung-out paterfamilias piloting a people carrier full of enfants terribles from the Dordogne to Calais. Work time, holiday time, both are

strictly delimited in the modern era, and all too often the interface between the two is the high-speed motorway drive.

It may be theoretically possible to leave the *péage* and meander off into the vineyards, there perhaps to seduce a numinous 'thou' with a flask of wine; but in practice embankments, cuttings and tunnels eradicate the soft contours of the landscape, while the cogs of the car tyres mesh with tarmac teeth to make 140 kmph forward motion as ineluctable as a funicular. Entrée . . . Mussidan, Sortie . . . Arveyres, PRIX . . . 5.70 euros. The little paper tongue licks the lobe of your ear with its patent insincerity: have you not just been winched over an ancient and venerable monoculture of great sophistication in a steel cask of unspeakable crudity? Are not you and your offspring merely a portion of that great human vendage, whereby the British bourgeoisie are squeezed out in the heart of France in the dying days of August?

St Emilion, Monbazillac, Saussignac . . . the great grapes are trampled by the whirling rubber of wrath and stress. Ferchrissakes! We just steamed past St Michel-de-Montaigne without so much as a sideways glance! What would the venerable essayist have made of this? His take on the world was compendious to the point of being encyclopaedic, but the closest he came to penning 'On *péages*' is his fragment 'On riding "in post"'. According to Montaigne, 'The Wallachians . . . make the fastest speeds of all . . . because they wear a tight broad band around their waists to stop them from tiring, as quite a few others do. I have found no relief in this method.' Nor me, nor me; even a conventional seatbelt is irksome after five hundred kilometres and a pit stop to peck on a reconstituted prong of pureed pig meat with a 6 euros prix fixe.

Still, at least the kids are holding up well as we whack up the A10 past Angoulême, Poitiers and Tours. Not for them the insistent jibing of this road to unfreedom. My mind drifts back to my own childhood, and family voyages in the Austin to Wales, embarked upon before the construction of the British motorway system. I recall it took days, as my father appeared to have been taught to drive at a purely theoretical level by Jean-Paul Sartre, and so regarded each depression of the accelerator as an existential leap into being. There was snow too, great drifts of it, out of which lorries lumbered looking like woolly mammoths.

My reverie is stirred up and then finally dispersed by the great dark lodestone of Paris. We leave the machine ensemble of the *péage*, only to be locked into another one: tens of thousands of cars inching forward in near-gridlock. It isn't until we've been stuttering along for over an hour that my thirteen-year-old vouchsafes that this is the day of the European athletics championship. It would be ironic, this joyless driving for hundreds of kilometres only to be held up by people fun-running, were it not that the true psychogeographer never experiences irony. 'See that,' says the lad, indicating the fragment of a map Michelin have put on the cover of their France 2003 Tourist and Motoring Atlas, 'd'you think they've put Brest on the front so that they'll sell more copies?' My heart swells with paternal affection: a psychogeographer in the making, n'est-ce pas?

# Apples or Pears?

A frozen moment at US Immigration, JFK Airport, New York. My British passport is scanned, the official scrutinises the computer screen with a worried expression and then politely asks me to go into the back room. I join what look like a hundred Koreans and a miscellany of other potential personae non grata. A Frenchman is being noisily grilled by an immigration officer at a high desk. The officer looks like an ugly, acne-scarred version of Jim Carrey, the Frenchman looks preposterous: fur-trimmed jeans, a leather patchwork shoulder bag, collar-length hair. Frankly, I wouldn't try to get in to Legoland looking like that – let alone post-9/11 America.

'You say you're a philosophy teacher,' the officer insinuates, 'in Grenoble, but you seem to spend an awful amount of time here.'

'Yez, like I say, I 'ave ze girlfriend.'

'Yeah, yeah, I know that, in Manhattan, and you're in and out of here like a yo-yo. There are stamps here,' he riffles the French passport, 'for every month of the last goddamn year.'

The Frenchman shrugs: 'She is my girlfriend.'

'Hey, whatever,' the officer is suddenly bored. He stamps the passport and beckons me up. 'Now, Mister Self, are there some little things you maybe aren't telling us about yourself?'

'Well,' my voice drawls from deep in clubland, 'there are perhaps one or two trifling drug offences, ancient history really.'

'We're going to have to deport you; you cannot come in on a visa waiver form with prior narcotics convictions. You'll have to go back to London and apply for a visa there.' My heart sinks then steadies.

'Look, officer,' I say, 'would it make any difference if I told you that I was an American citizen?'

The Jim Carreyalike scrutinises me intently. 'What makes you think that?'

I tell him that my mother was a citizen, born in 1922 in Columbus, Ohio, and that she registered me at the US Embassy in London when I was born. Carrey says he will check this information out, and shoos me back to the bolted-down seats.

Over the next two hours all the Koreans and some Africans with impressive cicatrisation scars are admitted to the Land of the Free. The only people left are me and a silently weeping German family, comprising late-middle-aged parents and a grown-up daughter. Apparently the paterfamilias failed to get an exit stamp in his passport when he departed in 1987. Jim Carrey and I have struck up an acquaintanceship; we suck mints together and listen to Miles Davis's *Kind of Blue* played on the CD-Rom drive of his computer terminal. Finally, he beckons for me to follow him and leads me back through a warren of offices. 'I'm taking you back here,' he confides, 'because we've decided to admit you, but we're going to deport the Germans and . . . ' he pauses significantly, 'I don't want to upset them any more than necessary.'

In the back office sits an older, heavier-set man with a strict moustache and iron-filing hair. The Stars and Stripes limps on the flagpole by his desk. He looks up from studying my passport when Jim and I enter.

'So, Mister Self,' he asks without preamble, 'what exactly do you think you are?'

'Um, well, a dual citizen, I suppose.'

He breathes heavily. 'Mister Self, I have been an immigration officer for thirty-five years and let me tell you something: you are either an apple or a pear.' He pauses, allowing this fructuous moment to dangle between us. 'I don't care if you choose to live in London, I don't even mind if you travel on a British passport when you're abroad, but let me tell you this,' his voice begins to quaver with emotion, 'when you come here to the United States of America you are an American citizen!'

I snap to attention. 'The Battle Hymn of the Republic' swells in my inner ear as I deftly circle my covered wagon in front of the Lincoln Memorial, leap out and march forward to receive the Pulitzer. 'Sir, yes sir!' I bark. On the way out Jim Carrey passes me my British passport.

'I don't even want to hold this,' his voice is also choked with patriotism, 'because it offends me to see you travelling on such a document.'

Now, a few months later, I am the proud possessor of an American passport, and to begin with I felt pretty strange about it. To tell the truth I've never felt my nationality defined me any more than my shoe size (actually, since my shoe size is 12, a good deal less), but since actualising my Americanness I've given a good deal of thought to whether I feel American, or British, or European – or anything. Am I in fact a citizen of a vast Oceania which stretches from Brest-Litovsk to Honolulu? But on consideration, weighing up all the geopolitical, historical and cultural factors, it's dawned on me that the possession of two passports means one thing and one thing alone: shorter queues on embarkation either side of the Atlantic. I'm not an apple or a pear, I'm a banana skin, glissading through immigration.

# High on Merseyside

Sitting in a soft-stripped flat on the twenty-first floor of a semi-abandoned tower block in the Kensington district of Liverpool I am temporarily the highest resident on Merseyside. I can see the sunlight dapple the flanks of Snowdon nigh on seventy miles to the south. I can see the Wirral like a spatulate tongue licking the Irish Sea. I can see the Mersey itself, coursing through its trough of defunct docks. Towards Bootle the gargantuan sails of wind turbines look like propellers powering the upside-down burgh through the steely grey sky. Ranged across the mid-ground are the signature buildings of the city: the Liver Buildings with their sentinel herons; the mucoid concrete of the hospital; the dirty white stalk of the radio station with its restaurant revolving like a conjuror's plate; and the two cathedrals, one the outhouse of the morally relativist gods, the other a split yoghurt pot oozing spiritual culture.

The grid of streets spreads out from the base of my tower, a tight stacking of tiled roofs which gleam wet with rain. I sit here from dawn to dusk watching the weather systems roll in, completely divorced from the human life of the city. The block will soon be demolished. Twenty years ago tens of these concrete snaggle teeth gnashed Liverpool's flesh – but they've mostly been extracted. Draughts sough in the empty corridors and cavernous stairwells. As the block is emptied out so is the city itself; and, despite endless talk of regeneration, the fact remains that Liverpool has halved in population since the second war. To apprehend this you have only to observe the slow trickle of outward-bound traffic which is the rush hour, or descend into the financial district at 5.30 p.m., where you'll find hardly anyone at all. The impressive Victorian municipal buildings lower in the dusk, stage sets for an epic long since wrapped.

Occasionally the Wirral is too tantalising and I grab my foldaway bicycle, sprint to the lift, plummet to the ground, freewheel all the way down the hill to the Pier

LYVER
BIRDMAN

81

Head and take the ferry across the Mersey. 'Ferry 'cross the Mersey!' sings Gerry over the tannoy, while the Pacemakers plink-plonk their accompaniment. This is a moment of maximum urban quiddity, the song hymning the vehicle while you're actually on it. It's like a busker singing 'Streets of London' in the streets of London, at once sweetly homely and infinitely claustrophobic. But all too soon we've heaved to at Seacombe and I'm pedalling along the magnificently sculpted Wallasey Embankment past the tidy villas of Egremont. On and on, the peninsula curving and curving to my left as I circumvent the last resort of New Brighton.

Empty sky, flat sea, sharp wind. The occasional lonely walker, head bowed to escape the oppression of the sky. If I felt alone in the echoing precincts of the city, I now feel completely abandoned. On the outskirts of Hoylake a fat middle manager sleeps off his expense account pub lunch slumped in his Ford Omega, while I take a piss in a public toilet acrid with fresh saltwater and ancient urine. I thought I might walk from the point across to the tidal island of Hilbre, there to commune with seals, but in the event my timing is wrong, so I cycle to the station, fold the bike up and take the train back into the centre.

At Birkenhead we descend clanking into the tunnel under the Mersey, and suddenly all is echoing expanses of white tiling, festoons of cabling, and glimpses of tortuous machinery which suggest the nightmare visions of Piranesi. Intended for a far larger population, the superb local rail system of Merseyside is housed in caverns beneath the city itself, a ghost train endlessly circumnavigating the interior of this dark star of urbanity. But as if these tunnels, and the Queensway road tunnel under the river, weren't enough of a vermiculation, in the last few years a group of enthusiastic volunteers have been opening up the Williamson tunnels. These brick-lined conduits were built by a local magnate during the early decades of the nineteenth century. Some say they were a labour-creating project, a piece of proto-Keynesianism, intended to provide employment for soldiers returned from the Napoleonic Wars. Others aver that Williamson himself was a millenarian, and that the tunnels were intended as a refuge for Liverpudlians from the coming apocalypse.

If the tunnels' genesis is in dispute, then so is their extent. Some claim there are only a few hundred metres of them, but others swear that the whole fabric of the city is riddled like a vast Emmental cheese. Whatever the truth of the matter, the tunnels are a curious complement to the depopulation of Liverpool, an introjection of the municipality's own sense of its emptiness; after all, if so many people have vanished, where can they possibly have gone to?

# The Holy City

I arrived in Varanasi by minibus, a stubby little eight-seater which clumped and bumped along the straight and rutted roads of Uttar Pradesh from the Nepalese border. It took three interminable and baking days, days I spent sitting opposite an Australian hippy wearing a Victorian nightdress. Having no humanity or fellow feeling whatsoever, he read aloud from Shakespeare's sonnets the whole way. I'll never compare anyone to a summer's day as long as I live, not after that.

Other passengers included a family of diminutive Indians. The pocket pater-familias wore a white shirt, string vest, pressed trousers and shined shoes; the mini-matriarch was sandalwood-scented in a silk sari; the young princeling sported an Aertex shirt, grey shorts and school sandals. They never seemed to sweat, this family; the flies never alighted on them. They took chapattis from one Tupperware box and scooped up dahl from another, yet no grease was left on their nimble fingers. Were they perhaps – I idly considered – coated in transparent Teflon?

The nights we spent in wayside caravanserai, where I sweated and boinged on unstrung charpoys. Grey dawn would find me as fatalistic as any native, and shamelessly shitting at the side of a field. The landscape was so unfinished and yet so used up, like a vast kitchen in which no one had troubled to do the washing up for several millennia. By the time we reached the Holy City I'd just about had enough of travelling. I booked into the government Tourist Bungalow and took to my bed. The room was an upended stone shoebox with nothing in it besides a mattress and a bare light bulb. Outside there was an ox park. All day long an Untouchable woman scraped up the dung and mounded it into a compact ziggurat which abutted the exterior wall of my room. When night came she lay down on top of it and we slept within arm's reach of one another.

After three supine days I ventured out. I'd met an excitable Ukrainian while sucking on bottles of Stag Ale in the Bungalow's restaurant. He told me that he was

in exile; his father – a high Soviet official – had sent him abroad to escape military service in Afghanistan. He believed in every conspiracy theory going: the Jews controlled the US and the USSR, while being controlled themselves by Venutians whose spacecraft was moored in the Bermuda Triangle. You could spot the aliens, he said, by their propensity for baldness and driving convertible Mercedes. On his old rucksack the wandering anti-Semite had the names of every country he'd visited, from Swaziland to Switzerland, crudely inscribed in ballpoint pen.

We went to the railway station so that I could buy a ticket for the Himigiri–Howrah Express, a mighty Aryan iron horse that would drag me clear across the north of the subcontinent to Chandigarh. I got a chitty from Window A and took it for authorisation to Window B. At Window B I received a second chitty and took it to the Sales Booth. Every single step had to be taken through a dense thicket of humanity; thorny limbs pricked me, twiggy fingers scratched me. I emerged blinking and bedevilled into the harsh light of the maidan. The Ukrainian examined my ticket and pointed out that I'd mistakenly bought one for the service which departed in eight days' time, rather than on the morrow. I considered the hour-long battle that would be required to change the ticket, and, taking my lead from the ideas of astrological propitiousness embodied in Indian culture, rather than the cult of horological precipitateness enshrined in my own, I determined to stay the extra seven days in the Holy City.

Another kulfi-headache dawn. I'd linked up with a Canadian Buddhist – the very worst kind. He propped me on the handlebars of his Supercomet bike and pedalled us both down to the bathing ghats. Downriver I could see smoke rising from the death barbecue: long pig griddling for breakfast. The Buddhist knelt and prayed angrily, while I shared a chillum with a crusty sadhu. There was grit in the air, grit on my eyes, grit in my retinal afterimages. The terracing of temples and shrines, the lapping brown limbs of the goddess Ganga – for some hazy, hashy reason it all reminded me of Brighton. So it seemed like a perfectly logical step to strip, wind a lungi around my snaky hips, and descend into the natal flow. Halfway across I collided with the corpse of a cow, which, bloated to four times its life size, revolved slowly in the viral current. I spluttered, coughed, and went under while ingurgitating spirochaetes to last me a lifetime.

All this happened twenty years ago and I'd like to say that it seems like yesterday, but it doesn't: it seems like twenty years ago. Now I'm an older, less adventurous and less stoned man. Nowadays I would change my ticket. Although, come to think of it, since my ultimate destination was Kashmir, I probably wouldn't be travelling there at all. The past is another country – and the frontier is always closed.

# The Chilterns

Slogging up through the woods and on to the main ridge of the Chilterns on a damp morning in late autumn, the joys of summer rambles seem long departed. Ah! If only I could recapture that fearless rapture with which I turned the golden key, wrenched open the door and ran laughing down the corridor into the Queen of Hearts' rose garden. Dandelion days! Sweet scattered spore of youth! When to the sessions of sweet silent thought we summon up . . . and so on and so forth, jaw-jaw, bore-bloody-bore. No, the fact is that it's pissing down and I'm a middle-class, middle-aged man making tea on a miniature gas stove in a tiny covert, while down the muddy track beside me ride upper-class middle-aged women on chestnut stallions exchanging the small change, the he-shagged-she-spat of hacking society.

But I've no time to get lost in such regrets. I'm on a mission. In my rucksack are enough uppers, downers, twisters and screamers to transmogrify the passive pheasants of these pleasant hills into the avian equivalent of suicide bombers. Strange Miles, my neuro-pharmacological consultant – who operates out of a light industrial estate near Princes Risborough – has been working on this gear all summer. He swears blind that if I leave enough of it in the feed bins scattered along the ridge, then come the first day of the shooting season, instead of doing the flying equivalent of ambling towards the wavering guns of a lot of tipsy City brokers, the fowl will rise up and descend in a fluttering, bombinating horde. Their target? Chequers.

I only hope the Prime Minister himself will be in residence that weekend and get espaliered by an thousand tiny beaks, but, if not, if he's in Texas or Timbuktu, then I'm prepared to accept whatever fatalities may be caused by the drug-crazed birds. Strange Miles and I simply see this as collateral damage in our two-man war against the entrenched power of the state.

On I slog and slide, the rich clayey soil spattering my nylon flanks. But what's this! Just past Cobblershill Farm I come across a folding table set up by the wayside.

87

A number of clingfilm-wrapped placards enjoin me to sign a petition against the use of this bridleway by four-wheel-drive vehicles. Of course I should sign! Every fibre in my being cries out against the desecration of the countryside by these disgusting vehicles . . . and yet . . . and yet . . . if I'm entirely honest I cannot deny that I myself have done a fair bit of off-roading. In the early 1990s, when I found myself temporarily marooned in a small cottage in deepest Suffolk, the green lanes beckoned to me with their cushioned camber and their soft verges.

Few people realise quite how many green lanes there are in England, let alone that you're allowed to drive cars along them. If I took the B roads back from the Ship Inn at Dunwich, or the Bell in Walberswick, to my cottage outside Leiston, there was always the slim chance that I might encounter one of the two patrol cars that cover East Anglia. Not that I would've been over the limit, you understand, it's just that encounters with the authorities of any kind have always given my sensitive nerves a dreadful jangle. No, much better to slide out of Walberswick and then across the common on the sandy, rutted, potholed track past the haunted hippy house. In deepest darkest winter there was always a tremendous frisson when I reached the last outpost of civilisation and doused the headlights. Proceeding by the light of the stars at a stately 5 mph, the wind battering the featherweight chassis of the little car, always made me feel that I'd stripped away all the useful accoutrements of motoring, to leave merely a locomotive residuum.

It helped that I was driving a Citroën Deux-Chevaux. Yes, not for me the padded monstrosity of a Toyota Land Cruiser or the effortless functionality of a Land Rover Discovery. Not for me the effortless traction of four massive tyres. What made my night-time green lane driving an acceptable form of transport, rather than a dubious kind of recreation, was that I allowed the countryside itself a fighting chance. True, the 2CV does perform very impressively in the rough, but there was always a good chance that I'd get myself bogged down and end up having to slog home twelve miles on foot. It happened several times – and I felt good about it. But these bastards ploughing the Chilterns into a furrowed morass, they simply shouldn't be allowed. I withdrew my tungsten carbide ballpoint from its oiled leather sheath and signed the petition with a flourish, before plopping on in the direction of Little Hampden.

A fortnight later the PM stepped out on to the ha-ha of Chequers in the lemony light of a perfect autumn morning. The shotgun reports up on the ridge sounded like the doors of so many suburban semis being precipitately slammed by hurrying commuters – or so he thought in a rare moment of metaphoric insight. And that cloud up there, what could it be? So many airborne motes fusing into coherence and then fissioning into chaos, like thoughts in a disordered mind.

# Madame Jacquard

James Fox doesn't so much smoke cigarettes as allude to the possibility of them being smoked. The fiery treat is sparked, two or three deep inspirations ensue, then the white trunk is fiercely coiled in the elephant's graveyard of the ashtray. Having observed James smoke for some time now I've been driven to consider anew how for the nicotine addict the act defines both time and space. One of the first things you notice when you give up cigarettes is how your previously linear narrative is translated into a series of perplexing jump-cuts. Just as journeys are no longer measured by the number you smoke – home to Tube, one; car to work, three – so the whole day loses its rudder and heels about hopelessly on the choppy surface of the era.

I suspect that James's manner of smoking has evolved over decades of global journalistic assignments. His is the prescient puffing of a man about to be airlifted out of Kigali shortly before the machetes begin to swish; his is the stolen suck which precedes the long walk down the air-conditioned corridor of power. By smoking an untipped Gitane in less than three minutes James ensures that his space-time continuum is rigidly defined, a blue-brown set that can be erected and then struck within seconds. But at what cost? While I've always maintained that to seek out cut-price tobacco for myself with any seriousness is a dangerous admission (if I have to economise, shouldn't I give up?), what's to prevent me helping James to budget more wisely?

In Britain the Exchequer ensures that James's preferred brand sets him back nearly twice as much as it would in its native France. I resolve to drive James to Calais to stock up; after all there's a certain satisfaction in joining the great exodus to avoid duty, especially if experienced vicariously. Hundreds of thousands of Britons take the cross-Channel ferry to buy cheap booze and fags in France (and, since the French have hoiked their own tax, in Belgium); just as Finnish hordes take the train to Russia to buy vodka, and Norwegians – I am reliably informed – troll

SMOKER'S CEILING—A Study in SEPIA

across to Sweden for cut-price sweeties. Doubtless perplexed archaeologists in the far future, discovering domestic middens of far-flung packaging, will hypothesise that the turn of the third millennium saw huge migrations of European peoples, each of them bringing their own distinctive material culture.

Rolling off the ferry in the afternoon darkness of mid-winter, James and I are sucked along as if I were piloting a spacecraft caught by a tracker beam. We bump over tram tracks and cobbles into the heart of Calais, skirt the Gothic asteroid of the Mairie and eventually dock in a busy thoroughfare. The shop fronts cosily glow; the good burghers of Calais, far from being enchained, are bustling about. At second-storey level we can see at least two of those distinctive elongated diamond-shaped signs which advertise the presence of a *tabac*.

In France the production, packaging and sale of tobacco is regulated by SEAT, the government monopoly, so these *tabacs* are as far from the British fag shop as is imaginable. In place of a Perspex rack offering a few tawdry filtered brands – with names like 'Hanover' and 'Plantagenet' – you're presented with a startling array of tobacco-as-confectionery, displayed on glass shelves, while cabinets contain pipes, lighters and other fumilanary implements. And this is only the window dressing, because every *tabac* is attached to a vast storehouse, within which are entombed whole divisions of cigarettes, those suicidal infantrymen of the war against humanity.

Such an emporium was the Tabac Jacquard, and I saw it intoxicate poor James. At my suggestion he bought enough Gitanes to make the trip feel worthwhile. Worthwhile financially – he saved £300 – but worthwhile spatio-temporally as well, because with four thousand cigarettes on board he had in an important way mapped out the course of the next five months. No more late-night pilgrimages to one tobacconist that sells his brand, no more unpleasant fermatas as the white metronomes stop ticking. As he made the calculations with La Divina Nicotina – who appeared to me as a dowdy Frenchwoman of a certain age – a faint flush crept into James's normally saturnine features.

When we regained the street James had two large carrier bags full of Gitanes and a sloppy grin on his face. He enthused over the gentility, the polish of the woman who he'd dubbed 'Madame Jacquard'. He fantasised about seducing her away from her husband and settling down in Calais with a little *tabac* of his own. A week later in London I chanced to look at the receipt for my own modest purchase at the Tabac Jacquard and discovered why it was so called: it's on the Rue Jacquard. But I haven't had the heart to ruin James's fictive relationship with Madame Jacquard. Not yet anyway.

# Zooming Moulay

Zooming Moulay had to have been a mistake. Granted, he was taking liberties, but it's one thing to zoom in your backyard, quite another to zoom cross-culturally. And what a culture to cross: Morocco, with its mystical secret fraternities, its a priori belief in the efficacy of practical magic, and its civilisation founded on successive waves of fanatical puritans emerging from the arid turbulence of the Sahara to stop everyone dancing. No, if you're going to zoom anyone abroad do it somewhere like Bavaria, or Belgium.

It's not even as if I didn't know what I was up against. I'd been in Marrakesh enough times to understand that while for a short stay it's sufficient to shout 'Je ne suis pas touriste, j'habite au casa!' to the legions of young men who descend on you like vultures the second you step outside your hotel, if you're staying much longer you're more or less under an obligation to employ a guide. The very least you can do if you're going to take a cheap holiday in someone else's misery is alleviate it just a little.

It may have been that Moulay disliked my set-aside scheme for him. I made it clear that I didn't require his guiding skills at all, but was content to give him a per diem just to keep the other flapping djellabas off my back. That and a little shopping, for majoun (marijuana mixed with dates and honey to make an edible confection), and Spanish Fly (actually dried beetles of the genus Lytta vesicatoria). I thought I was letting him off lightly, but Moulay kept insisting on guiding me through the tortuous passageways of the old town, press-ganging me into this mosque or that tannery. Clearly what I was giving him wasn't sufficient – he needed to make his kickbacks from other operators.

Eventually I found myself in the ridiculous situation of trying to dodge my own guide. I'd duck out of the hotel, leap in the car, swirl into the Jama Al F'na in a cloud of dust and take up my position in the Cosmos Café, looking out over the sun-beaten square at the snake charmers, the steaming food stalls and the wild Berber men in from the Atlas hawking their wares. But inevitably Moulay would surface at my elbow within seconds of my arrival, as if telepathically informed of my presence. This attribute of his alone should've warned me against zooming him.

Ah, Moulay, with his fake Dolce & Gabbana shades and his queasy grin: I thought I knew him then, understood his straightforward rapaciousness, but I was a prize chump. It was the second batch of majoun that decided me. The first was forgivably small, but the second was titchy. I and my companion had necked the lot, crunched all the cantharides, and still felt no more aroused than a couple of pensioners eating potted shrimps at Prestatyn. (Actually, knowing as I do the almost legendary sexual appetites of the Welsh, probably a great deal less aroused.) When I challenged Moulay about this he was much aggrieved: 'It is too strong for you to eat more majoun, you westerners cannot cope with it . . . I am protecting you . . .' Protecting me, my foot. I insisted that we rendezvous at the hotel the following morning; for once I had somewhere I wanted him to guide me.

If he looked shifty and dog-eared in the early morning, I probably looked a good deal worse. I got him into the car, one of those Renault 4s that the Moroccans – out of some misplaced romanticism – insist on referring to as 'scorpions of the desert'. We drove to a café where I rolled the last of the Sputnik hashish I'd bought in Tangier into a joint the size of a baby's forearm. Over mint tea I made sure that he smoked as much of it as I, and by the time we left his eyes were two red deltas of blood vessels. Back in the car I told him our destination: 'I want to go to the old Jewish Quarter.' 'Yes, yes,' he acceded, 'that's no problem, I will take you there.' My foot rammed the accelerator to the floor and we shot away. I drove the scorpion through town as if we were on an extempore leg of the Paris to Dakar Rally, hurling the tip-tilting car this way and that. Moulay clutched the sides of his seat. I fancied I could even sense the mint tea rising in his gorge. He could barely raise a shaky hand to indicate the way.

In the Jewish Quarter I demanded a Jew. 'Why? Why do you want to speak to these people?' He was already half-zoomed. 'Because I'm a Jew myself, Moulay – I want to speak with my people. This city used to have a big Jewish community – I want to know what happened.' To his credit, Moulay found me a Jew, and a Jewish dentist to boot. The dentist and I sat in his dusty surgery under a diorama of curiously garish posters depicting dental caries. He spoke in Arabic and Moulay interpreted: He was an elderly man. Most of the Jews had left Morocco; they'd gone to Israel like one of his sons, or to the States like one of his other sons. His wife was

93

dead. The seconds ticked away in the wounded mouth of the surgery: the Jews of Marrakesh had been extracted.

Back in the street Moulay seemed fully zoomed, and I left him standing there. We didn't see him for the last few days we spent in Marrakesh, but I've seen him

since, oh yes indeed. Whenever I feel uneasy or out of my depth in a foreign country, Moulay is always on hand to offer me his services. He appears in my dreams, his sunglasses opaque, his smile queasy, a relentless reminder of the truth that you should never zoom a Moroccan.

# Decoys in Iowa

In Iowa the land is flat and the people are fat. Like petrol-driven bowling balls they roll across the plains, occasionally slotting into the groove of a roadway, then rattling to a halt at fast-food joints where they are served with paper cups of 7 Up or Coke the size of oil drums, haystack hamburgers and stooks of fries. In Iowa the land is flat, and divided into a crinkly chessboard of farms. The towns have names derived from just about every other conceivable land – Lisbon, Oxford, Bangor, Lourdes, Fredonia – mixed together with curiously modern coinages – Mechanicsville, Urbandale – so that the state's identity is an invented palimpsest, worked up out of elsewhere. In Iowa it's fall, and the tawny stands of brush along the river beds fade to grey, while the yawning maw of the sky cries out for geese to gobble and duck to crunch.

The great American stand-up Steven Wright has a gag: 'Last year I bought a map of the USA, actual size. This year for my vacation, I folded it.' I think he was thinking of the Midwest when he came up with this.

At Cedar Rapids Airport the boy and I rent my usual sloppy General Motors coupé. 'Make it as sloppy as possible,' I tell the girl at the Alamo desk. 'I want that transmission to feel like a slack rubber band, and the suspension to make the car handle like a manatee wallowing in the Everglades.' She looks at me askance – which is a difficult thing to do if you're an Iowan, what with fat eyeballs an' all. 'We've a day to kill,' I continue. 'What is there worth seeing in this neck of the woods?' To the girl's credit she rises to the occasion: 'I can recommend the Amana Colonies, sir,' she says, 'out on Route 151. They're real inneresting . . .' ('Real inneresting': to my ear it sounds like a state of Buddhist contentment) '. . . there's exhibits, and the old houses where they lived – it was a religious community one time – and there's good stuff to eat.'

Eat, yeah, I know your game. Still, it sounds good to me. I'd drive miles to see the remains of any old godforsaken religious community so long as there's a gift

shop. But the boy is tugging at my sleeve: 'Dad, don't forget . . .' 'Oh yes,' I turn back, 'what about a mall? My boy here wants to visit a nice big mall.' 'The biggest mall hereabouts is down at Coralville, sir, right on Route 380, you just head right on from the Amana Colonies.' 'Well, we'll do that then.' 'You have a nice day, sir.'

The coupé is as sloppy as a blancmange and I smear it along the road past prosperous farms with silvery grain silos and four-square red barns. Occasionally we pass a mirror-shiny tanker and I see the coupé, me and the boy reflected in its fat belly. The Amana Colonies are nothing much to look at: a few clapboard houses full of Germanic heirlooms, a handful of barns scattered with bits of old farming equipment. The Amana were, it transpires, socialistic and pious. They were resistant to modernity, but not quite resistant enough – so the combine harvester of Progress crushed them flat and rolled right over them.

In this neck of the woods you have to be truly outlandish to survive as a religious sect. You have to be like the Amish and reject even the button. The Amish are so out there that the word is they're heavily stuck into the drugs trade in Des Moines. Not that they use the stuff themselves, you unnerstand; it's just that, what with farm prices falling, and the Gentiles so hungry for the stuff, it has to be one of God's ways of providing for the Chosen.

We eat in the restaurant at Amana. It looks like the sort of joint that would be made out of gingerbread in a Grimm Bros. production, and the food is all sugar and fat to match this. The boy can't handle it – and who can blame him? He longs only for Coralville and the promised mall. Back in the coupé we noodle through Homestead and Oxford, then pull up in the humungous car park next to the retail behemoth.

The mall was worth the journey. It's so big it has a multiplex, an ice rink, numerous cafés and retail outlets arrayed along what seems like half a kilometre of temperature-controlled atrium. But most alluring of all is the gun store. This is what the boy really wanted to see: hundreds of shooting rifles, handguns, semi-automatic weapons, and all the ammunition to go with them. For a Brit boy it's simply inconceivable that this much firepower can be available in what, to all intents and purposes, looks like suburbia.

I call his attention to the fact that we're out in the sticks really, and that behind every one of them crouches a proud American who is crazy for the hunt. I point out to him the flotillas of decoy ducks and geese, the foldaway boats, the self-assembling hides, but he isn't fooled for a second. He's seen those Iowans, those great big, lumbering Iowans, who are themselves like decoy humans: bigger than life size so as to confuse their enemies; fool them into misjudging their descent, so that when they try and join them, they crash instead into the iron-hard ground.

# Business as Usual

The impact of civil disturbance on the built environment is a source of pure joy for even the most conformist of salarymen and women. An external threat to a city, whether in the form of armies of lovelorn Greeks, Nazi bombardiers or even DIY suicide bombers, serves to shore up the great bulwark of temporal power; but when the citizenry themselves loft bricks into the state apartments and take torches to the bureaucracy, then only the most hardened of hearts can remain unmoved.

Most ancient cities are constructed around a citadel, within which the powers that be can retreat in times of riot, taking with them their idols and their gods. However, in the modern era these Kremlins have been replaced with broad boulevards, too wide for barricades, and allowing a clear line of fire for artillery. An important part of urban renewal has always been securing lines of retreat for despots and demagogues. Don't be fooled by all that tommyrot about affordable housing: look at Paris, for Christ's sake.

London owes its status as the seat of the oldest extant representative government in the world as much to its riot-friendly squares and tortuous roadways as it does to any real democracy. The London mob has always revelled in its ability to strike total fear into the apparatchiks, whether Royalists, Parliamentarians or New Labourites. A fact often passed over in silence is that we have a singular act of immolation to thank for the neo-Gothic monstrosity of the current Palace of Westminster. The old Palace was burnt down in 1834 when the elm-wood sticks, once used to record the accounts of the Court of Exchequer, were disposed of in the furnace beneath the House of Lords. The London mob, doubtless admiring of this auto-destruction, stood watching the conflagration and cheering in a jolly, Dickensian fashion.

Each age of London has had the mob it deserves, from muscular apprentices running amok in the City to face-metal-sporting anti-capitalists (a curiously oxy-

moronic allegiance) fitting the statue of Winnie with a turf toupee. Last year's massive anti-war rallies turned Hyde Park into some occidental version of the Kumbha Mela, as untold thousands of provincial liberals gathered on the banks of the Serpentine to worship the general secretaries of schismatic unions. Crowds and mobs dislocate urban space, rendering the familiar outlandish and transmogrifying innocent pieces of street furniture into potentially lethal weapons. My God! you wail internally, I'm about to be kebabed on a litter bin by a straining phalanx of vegetarians!

The most exciting événement I've ever been caught up in was the Poll Tax riot of March 1990. Somewhat perversely – and apolitically – I'd taken the Tube into town to see a movie. I can't remember which movie it was, but I do recall that it was set in a desert, and I was looking forward to swapping breezy springtime London for a baking and sable expanse. Instead, I popped out of the intestines of the city to discover the West End in full fart. I was emerging on to the Charing Cross Road at exactly the time when the Metropolitan Police had lost control of the rioters in Trafalgar Square and were retreating in an orderly fashion in the direction of Cambridge Circus. So measured and theatrical was the riot that I had time to appreciate the way the police formed up into small shielded testudos, lost ground, broke, then reformed, as bottles and bricks crashed down on Plexiglas.

The rioters had got hold of scaffolding poles – which I thought a tad outré – and were doing their best to skewer the constabulary, but despite what was a quite desperate situation, the mounted police – presumably frightened out of their wits – were marshalling the crowds in the side streets in inimitable fashion. One reined his mount in front of me and said: 'Would you terribly mind moving back a little bit, sir?'

Meanwhile, in the Angus Steakhouse international citizens of the salad bar were munching their sirloins and sitting so placidly on their rumps that I felt the Last Trump might not disturb them. The police rallied outside the Porcupine pub on the opposite side of the road, and the drinkers who'd come out to see the action stepped casually to one side, incapable of apprehending the irony that they were standing, glasses in hands, while others were throwing them. It was then that I saw the tall, shaven-headed hipster who only two days earlier had cut my hair in a trendy hairdresser's, in a basement on Berwick Street Market. Resplendent in a leather car coat, he and a couple of pals had created their own mini-barricade out of some plastic milk crates and were crouched behind it snapping the action through phallic telephoto lenses.

It seemed so just, so very cusp-of-the-1990s, this club-culture civil disturbance with its ecstatic voyeurs, masked class warriors and amiable plods. In due course the whole remorseless farrago moved on up to Tottenham Court Road, where it dissipated in the shattered afterimages of plate glass, and the city resumed its normal state of pathological disregard.

# Canary Dwarf

In Dublin the big black Mercedes oozes through the mid-morning traffic. The atmosphere is greenish, submarine, as if the dregs of a gigantic pint of Guinness were being swilled about the Georgian terraces and squares. I haven't been here for seven years, and before that visit not since the early 1980s; this gives me a jump-cut perspective on the city's mutant growth: the wedges of steely contemporaneity hammered into its crumbling façade are blindingly obvious, whereas if I'd visited more frequently they would've insinuated themselves without my noticing.

'See that,' says Vivian, the driver, indicating three ten-storey, pyramidically roofed office blocks on the further bank of the Liffey. 'We call that Canary Dwarf.'

'That's right,' puts in Cormac, my companion, 'and you see the big spike thing over there . . .' he indicates a seventy-five-metre-high bodkin plunged into the urban pincushion, '. . . it's the Millennium Spire. When they were putting it up they had a giant crane sited right in front of Cleary's, the department store, then when they were finally finished everyone walked round town singing "I can see Cleary's now the crane is gone".'

It's a fitting entry to the westernmost cockpit of European literary modernism, this dinky-ville, in the grip of a painful dialectic between Catholicism and hedonism, and hence preoccupied with dualistic punning. The youthful populace of Dublin are being sucked out of the churches by the ideological vacuum; on to the streets, then into the bars and restaurants which have colonised the city centre. Where once burly men in soutanes enforced the creed, now burly men in black overcoats enforce the guest list. The curly plastic pigs' tails dangling from their bruised ears presumably allow them to hear the word of the nightclubbing god.

It's the brink of Ireland's presidency of the European Union and a cavalcade of pols are in town to jaw-jaw. At the mouth of every side street in the city centre steel barriers have been placed to provide leaning room for Gardai. So every car journey

we take – and we take many – proceeds at the stately pace of a sedan chair. 'There's roadworks in St Stephen's Green,' Vivian vouchsafes. 'They're putting in the new light railway line for the Luas.'

'Luas?' I query.

'It means something in Gaelic,' Cormac interjects, 'possibly "light".'

'Possibly,' Vivian continues, 'although most people call it the Lose, because so much bloody money has been spent on the thing.'

Money: this is the true Blarney Stone of Dublin – kiss it and you'll talk all night. The city is awash with wonga. The old public housing in the centre of town is being siphoned off, and the inhabitants poured into the big housing estates out by the ring road, which Dubliners don't hesitate to call 'ghettos', estates that are also home to black and brown faces. Immigrants to Ireland! The world is turned upside down; a country that's been sucked dry for four centuries is finally filling up again. Meanwhile, desirable residences are changing hands for astronomical figures: 450,000 euros for a tiny terraced house. Yes, the Eurotrash are in town, and one of the old Dublin city bosses is under judicial investigation – together with his pals – for taking kickbacks from developers going back to the 1960s. It's a friendly visit from Big Corruption to Little Graft, to show them how it's done.

Out at the headquarters of RTE they're shooting *First City*, the soap opera that keeps the state broadcasting network afloat. In among the anonymous four-storey blocks of knobbly concrete and green-tinted glass, the set is a coruscating notch. Bright lights pick out the frontage of a typical Dublin 'burb: a convenience store, a betting shop, and Phelan's, the bar that's the focal point for the drama. 'The fictional location is called Carrickstown,' Cormac says, 'but I'm pretty sure it's meant to be Crumlindrumagh down on the coast to the south of town.' It's a nice architectural prolepsis, this set: the old Dublin community lost in the concrete canyon.

That night we breast the rivers of light that the city streets have become. I remember being here in 1980 when the roadways were dark troughs after 11.00 p.m. Is it my faulty recollection, or were there also horse-drawn carts jolting over the cobbles? Now we sit in an echt eatery, inhaling Thai seafood. The couple beside us pay their bill and leave. 'See that woman,' Cormac says. 'I was at college with her. I kept trying to catch her eye, but the man with her wasn't her husband.'

'Yes,' puts in Peter, a fellow journalist who's dining with us, 'ours is the first Irish generation who've been able to commit adultery. We have the facilities, we have the opportunities. Still, in a town as small as this you're mad going to a restaurant.'

'Mad,' Cormac muses, contemplating the terrifyingly tiny world of the urban adulterer that Dublin's been dragged into.

# The Hot Spirit
## of the Caribbean

In Montserrat the hills mounted up to the volcano in a series of green gushes: plantations of bananas and sugar cane were interrupted by the painterly strokes of field terraces. This was a veritable Trevi Fountain of a Caribbean island, with at its summit a burbling fumarole which emitted a sulphurous stench, as the Devil tossed and turned beneath the earth's crust, farting off his evil business lunch.

I say was, because, of course, since I was there twenty-eight years ago the volcano has blown its top and submerged two-thirds of the island in its fiery dung. Gone is the miniature capital with its dinky colonial buildings, gone are most of the dusty hamlets I remember caroming through with my mother in our hire car; and, while we're at it, gone as well is my mother. I concede I can't make too much of this annihilation of a month of my adolescence by an earthy eructation, but there is something peculiarly distancing about the past no longer being another country, but instead a barren land.

I think back to the black volcanic sand beaches of the island that toasted the soles of my feet and can hear the jingle of the local radio station well in my inner ear: 'Got a feeling deep inside / It's a feeling I can't hide / Feel the spirit, feel it! / Feel the spirit of the Ca-ri-bbe-an / Radio Antilles, the big RA!' It was my mother's brother, Uncle Bob, who brought us to Montserrat. A one-time bigwig advertising man on Madison Avenue, Bob was responsible for – among many other things – the creation of the Pilsbury Dough Boy. A bakery burnout, followed by a triple heart bypass, drove him into early retirement. He and my aunt lived in a beautiful bungalow in one of the white retirement cantonments that studded the eastern shore of the island.

Uncle Bob may have furred up his ticker with fatty deposits but he wasn't sub-dued by guerrilla surgery. Without wishing to impugn his memory, I think it fair to say that Bob remained spectacularly choleric. Aged fourteen, I was set by my

uncle to clean the leaves from the gutters of the bungalow. After doing the back of the house, I moved to the front and saw him circling the poolside below, long-handled net in hand, as he fanatically removed particles of detritus from the pristine water. The inevitable mischievousness ensued: I dropped a single leaf from the roof into the pool and Bob swooped on it. I dropped a second and he swooped on this as well; a third followed and then a fourth. Finally, his hooded eyes tracked the path the leaf had followed back up to where I crouched, skinny on the eaves. With an almighty bellow of rage he smashed the pool scoop against the French windows, raced through the house, leapt into his Mini Moke and hurtled off into the hills.

But apart from these eruptions my uncle was a benign presence. The heart surgery hadn't stopped him smoking either, and he turned a blind eye as I swiped packets of State Express 555 from the yellow and gold cartons that were scattered about the house like flammable ingots. On Radio Antilles the advert went something like this:

'Daddy, why do you smoke State Express 555?'

'I smoke them, son, because they're the taste of success.'

'Daddy, when I grow up I'm going to smoke State Express 555.'

'You do that, son.'

With my State Express 555s well secreted I would be dropped off at the beach for a day's snorkelling. Flipper-flapping out over the ruched seabed, imprisoned in my own portable, aquamarine diorama, I would dive down twenty and even thirty feet for sand dollars. Then I'd swim out still further and round the point until I reached the reef. Multicoloured fish would explode from its gnarled contours, while in the periphery of my vision I could see blunt-nosed barracuda, tracking the incursion of what to them must've been a curious white amphibian. I don't imagine I'd be as sanguine now, but at fourteen I swam far out into the sea, revelling in the sight of manta rays the size of billiard tables, with their lethally poisonous queues-for-tails.

One day, with members of the Montserrat Walking Club, we walked up to the fumarole and stood staring into its stinky aorta. At the time it meant little to me, this fistula in the chest of Ceres, but now I wonder if Uncle Bob's longevity – he died this year aged eighty-six – owed something to his sojourn on Montserrat? He ended his days in North Carolina, but perhaps his regular rendezvous with the volcano in the 1970s and '80s allowed him to draw on its immense reserves of hot temper and so keep himself both alive and kicking.

# Fujian Mind Warp

The nineteen Chinese who died cockling in Morecambe Bay this February must have been hideously disorientated. The mile-wide sands, crossed by the channels of two rivers and networked with rivulets, are notoriously confusing; the tide also behaves here with fatal capriciousness, ebbing and flowing in patterns which can only be apprehended by those who've had years of experience. I was up on the fringes of the bay in January and even a brief walk along the sands, leaning at a forty-five-degree angle into the spume-laden gale, was enough to convince me that this was no place for anyone not powerfully motivated – desperate, even. As I plodded towards them flocks of oystercatchers lifted off into the vortical wind, where they were spun about like myriad items of tiny black and white laundry. Strange sand carts pulled by kites whipped about me, while on shore the windows of a giant old people's home were whited out by filmy cataracts of net curtain.

But what must it have been like for the Chinese? On the far side of the world from their natal homes in Fujian province, spending short nights crammed like sardines in vans parked in the dunes, before being turfed out, in darkness, to sieve the damp sand for a mollusc they'd never heard of before. There was no justification for this, no cultural swell of atavistic jellied memory to send them in pursuit of Cockles (and Mussels) Alive, Alive O. Then they found themselves caught between advancing walls of water with no way back to dry land, and so died, choking on their own disorientation.

Rather than engage with the existential horror of their demise, the British media preferred to treat of the Chinese's tragedy in purely economic terms. Whether classed as illegal immigrants or asylum seekers, their penury was the ostensible reason for their death, not the fact that they didn't know where they were. So disgustingly orientated were the news agencies that they were able to despatch reporters to

Fujian within hours of the tragedy, so that they could present to us highly accurate images of the forsaken place.

Those Chinese drowned in Morecambe Bay; the other Chinese suffocated in the lorry parked at the Dover ferry port; the Africans who plummet from the undercarriages of intercontinental jets as they make their approach to the developing world – am I alone in seeing all of these people as victims of extreme disorientation? Can we not go further and see that the attitudes of all Little Englander NIMBYists are merely a function of their privileged orientation? Knowing their place makes them determined to preserve it against all-comers. Or so they think, because in truth there are many among them who haven't got a clue where they truly are. Chop down the hedge, grub out the rhododendrons, warp the way markers and steal the route map from the glove compartment of their car, then they'd be floundering as forlornly as any cockle coolie.

Frankly, I think David Blunkett* should impose an orienteering test along with his citizenship exam; moreover, I think this should be retroactive, so that even those of us who've lived here all our lives should be obliged to pass, or else face expulsion. I propose this in the full knowledge that I myself might well be in severe difficulty. As I sit here, looking out over the rooftops of south London towards the giant glass Gherkin which now constitutes my most obvious point of orientation, I think I'm facing east. But I'm not 100 per cent certain of this, any more than I'm convinced of where I'm headed as I turn left out of my own front door. For most of us our social, political and economic orientation completely obscures where we are geographically. We live out our lives in cities that blot out natural features, while we resort to mechanical transport to annihilate distances and gradients. Disorientation is a luxury that only we in the affluent West can truly afford.

A fellow psychogeographer of mine – let's call him X – has been driving his wife slowly insane for years now with a creepy mind warp. Every time he drives her to the supermarket, in order to torment her with the fact of her disorientation he takes a slightly longer route. The journey can now take anything up to an hour (it should be no more than twenty minutes), and if she has the temerity to complain he merely informs her that it's a new shortcut. I point out to X in no uncertain terms, that, while his wife may have lost her sense of direction, he's abandoned any sense of proportion. Both of them are now floundering in the quicksand of a failed marriage, while the treacherous tide of mortality races inexorably towards them.

---

* Then British Home Secretary.

OYSTERS—
YES!
COCKLES—
NO....

ORIENT=DISORIENT Ralph STEADman 2004

# Côte of Desire

The Côte d'Azur isn't really a place at all – more a state of mind stretched out over hundreds of kilometres of beaches, headlands, outcrops, fish restaurants, walled villas and foul-tempered chiens. This sun-soaked coastline is like the strap of a bikini, suntan-oiled then teased by the imagination. My parents borrowed a house one winter at Cap d'Antibes. I was two years old and a precocious enough consumer to complain vociferously at receiving only a red plastic train for Christmas. I remember eating oysters; a palm tree growing in a courtyard; my mother collecting sea-smoothed chunks of coloured glass on the beach. She put her bounty in jars filled with water which she placed on the windowsills of the villa; the wintery sun shone through these stained-glass canisters.

Like all exotica experienced in earliest childhood, the South of France became entangled in my mind with its representations. Was it Willie Maugham who entertained at Cap Ferrat – or me? Was it Scott and Zelda who wheeled their Bugatti along the Corniche – or me? The swaddled figure scratching away in his notebook on the beach at Bandol, was it Thomas Mann, or, yet again, me? Hemingway and Picasso fighting on a canvas ring in the market square of Juan-les-Pins (where my lovely goes to, tra-la-la-la-la-la-la!); Truffaut and Bardot sunning themselves on Ari's yacht; Cézanne reducing the rocks to savage geometric configurations; Maigret nosing about Porquerolles savagely puffing on his pipe. Me, me, me, me-me-me!

So when I actually got to go there in early adulthood the experience remained curiously unreal, not least because I was under the auspices of louche Anglo-French aristos. We ate long lunches at restaurants in perfectly conical medieval hilltop villages, then drove to Les Calanques and dove off the white stone ledges into the inky Mediterranean. Or else we fetched up in Cassis, and after downing the requisite langouste quadrille, took the bizarre little mock submarine, which, semi-submersed, pedaloed across the harbour, affording us obscure views of the reefs of old Evian bottles on the seabed.

Bouillabaisse royaume was eaten at Le Brusc, in a giant glassed-in restaurant, itself not unlike a fish tank; and frankly the French bourgeoisie stuffing their faces were quite as ugly as the fish in the stew. There were promenades along the beachfront at Bandol, and on one memorable occasion we dropped acid and crossed over to the queer little island of Bendor. This blob of land was owned by a pastis millionaire and had been tricked out as a concrete Moorish fantasia, all crenellated courtyards and wonky minarets. In truth, Bendor was so bizarre that it quite neutralised the effect of the LSD; and it wasn't until we were back in Bandol, at one of those café-bars that charges forty quid for a vitelline-hued cocktail in a glass the size of a vitrine, that I remembered I was hallucinating.

My friends knew the by then venerable Logical Positivist Freddie Ayer, who had a house in the vicinity, and he much impressed me by his remorselessly rational impression of the world. When asked what single thing reminded him most of Paris, he thought for a while before answering: 'A road sign, with "Paris" written on it.' I savoured this remark, and in a way it was one of the seeds that eventually grew into the gnarled tree of my own psychogeographic preoccupations.

But eventually strolls in pine-scented woods and thyme-reeking maquis palled. There just wasn't the impetus required for even one more game of table football in the local bar. We were young, we had a sports car, we demanded bright lights and glittering debauchery. We decided to drive to Milan. We took off along the *péage* at 120 mph, whipping past Toulon, Hyères, St Tropez and Nice, before slowing to a crawl for the border crossing at Menton. Here, only yards before reaching Italy, we picked up a hitchhiker, a guileless local lad who'd just gone out for a stroll. Whipped up by our on-the-road fervour he determined to accompany us and drove us insane across northern Italy playing his guitar and singing old Crosby, Stills, Nash & Young songs.

On the way back the following night, pie-eyed by excess, we were pulled up before recrossing the border by one of those comic-operetta Italian policemen, all side-striped jodhpurs and a hat like a piece of shiny black leather origami. In those far-off pre-EU days papers were required, and, while we had ours, the poor strolling player had none, so without ceremony he was extracted from the jump seat and dragged away into custody. For some minutes we sat in the orange darkness and debated whether or not we should do something, but we were young and feckless and frightened, so we floored it and drove on. Besides, the whole trip had partaken of the dreamlike character of the Côte; and even now, more than twenty years later, I still find it hard to believe that the hitchhiker really existed at all.

SECOND-HAND BUGATTI-

OS OWNER Ralph Steadman 2004

# Be Here Now

In Chicago the boy wants to go up the Sears Tower. Of course, it's a mere 110 storeys high, and has long since been eclipsed by other vast edifices in the Near and Far East, but, still, it's there, we're there, he wants to make the ascent. I don't know exactly where these bigger buildings are, any more than I know precisely how high the Sears Tower is. Nevertheless, I picture these loftier skyscrapers as being shaped like colossal bodkins and darning mushrooms; crudely forceful examples of how reinforced steel and glass can be shaped to form the most prosaic of objects, then writ large, stupidly gross.

The Riyadh Bodkin and the Kuala Lumpur Mushroom are positive Meccas for all kinds of daredevils – of this much I'm sure. Decadent Saudi princes pilot microlights through huge holes in their façades, while Malaysian spider men scale them using giant suckers in lieu of crampons. All these activities serve to demonstrate is that modernist megaliths have completely suborned the role of natural features in providing us with the essential and vertiginous perspective we require to comprehend accurately our ant-like status. Natch.

My brother, who's an eminent architectural historian, often observes that the highest building to be erected during any given economic cycle is invariably a harbinger of recession. One thinks of Canary Wharf before the downturn in Britain of the 1990s, or the Twin Towers in New York before the shit hit the fan in the early 1970s. Come to think of it (and I am thinking of it a lot as we glide up Wells Avenue, the gale off Lake Michigan turning our socks into windsocks), the terrorist attacks of 9/11 may well doubly confirm this thesis by actually inducing a recession. Like so much in this brave new century, the economic edifice theory seems like an example of over-determination: 'too-true, too-true', a wise owl might coo.

Yes, I'm thinking about it a lot because it's only forty days since the WTC imploded, and the boy and I are adrift like autumn leaves in a chastened, muted

America. I admire the way his youthful enthusiasm segues with his lack of neurotic superstition. Sadly, the management of the Sears Tower don't see it that way and have closed the observation deck. The security men stare at us as if we'd asked to get on top of them – not just their building. But nevertheless they're happy enough to direct us the blowy mile back over the Chicago River and down Michigan Avenue to the John Hancock Center, which – while only a mere ninety-odd storeys – is still open for business.

I went up the WTC in 1993; I've been up the Empire State as well. The Eiffel Tower hosted me when I was eleven – the same age as the boy. Indeed, I've usually scaled the highest building in any city I've visited. In the States it's de rigueur for your hosts to whip you up one soon after your arrival, so that the descent into the airport followed by the ascent by lift feel curiously like the two sides of a rollercoaster's parabola. Nonetheless, it isn't the 1,000-footers that I find the most intimidating. Hedged round with their ordinary mystique – people work here for chrissakes! – they are also quite simply too high to provoke vertigo. Peering down from such a peak perspective only ever reduces the world below to an intelligible version of itself: the microcircuitry of society.

Still, on this particular dark day, full as it is with harbingers of mortality, the obsidian bulk of the John Hancock Center looks altogether threatening, as does the clanking lift lobby. Some of the lifts are out of order and shrouds of plastic have been taped across the entrances to these steely tombs. On the long ride up we stand together with a bog-ordinary quartet of out-of-towners – regulation moustaches, baseball caps, cameras and avoirdupois – and I wonder at their sang-froid. Could these couples be disciples of Epicetus, who've undertaken this purgatorial sightseeing purely in order to cultivate stoic detachment? Or are they merely dumb hicks?

Up on the observation deck we can feel the whole mass of steel, concrete, stone, plastic, fibre-optic cable and nylon carpet heal beneath us, as if it were a tall ship about to tack off across the crumpled grey surface of the lake, which curves away to the horizon. Like Prometheus I'm bound to this rock while the eagles of anxiety gnaw at my liver. The boy has no such problem. He scoots about from info point to info point; for him it's enough to be here now. There's a place where you can go out on to an enclosed terrace and promenade in the screeching elements, so naturally I force him to do the walk. Now it's his turn to feel fear – and mine to experience catharsis. It occurs to me that terrorism is Schadenfreude taken to the point of evil.

# Spin City

In the winter of 2001, my friend John and I were in Konya, central Anatolia, to attend the Mevlevi Festival where the dervishes famously whirl. There had been much derision concerning the festival in the tourist literature we'd read. Apparently the 'dervishes' weren't the real, impoverished, Sufi thing, but mere hirelings. It was true that the gig was held in a basketball stadium and appeared to be sponsored by a Turkish washing-machine company called Arçelik, but for all that the whirling quite spun us out. There was this, and there was the general austerity of cold-comfort Konya, a city of half a million-odd souls in the grip of Ramadan, as literally dry and dusty as it was metaphorically dry. John, having downed the sole can of beer provided in his minibar within an hour of arrival, tiptoed softly along the corridor to tap on my door and cop mine.

One evening we were sitting in the lobby of our hotel, the Balikçilar, a heavy joint – all shiny marble and knobbly stonework – when the divan we were sitting on was kicked by the gods from beneath. It felt as if this chunky leatherette banquette had transmogrified into a waterbed. The quake lasted for about a minute, then the lobby emptied in seconds – this was a region where people knew about earthquakes – and John and I found ourselves standing on a roundabout idly contemplating a bizarre bed of decorative cabbages.

At the time the tremor failed to impinge. After all, we'd been in the grip of vicarious religious fervour ever since arriving in Turkey. It wasn't until the following evening, after a three-hundred-kilometre drive into Cappadocia, when we saw on the BBC World Service that the earthquake had felled a minaret back in Konya and killed six people. I now found myself in the bizarre position of having escaped death in a natural disaster, only to be informed of the fact by people a thousand miles away in the Aldwych.

But, anyway, Cappadocia itself was also bizarre. This was an unleavened landscape

CAPPADOCIA *Velvet Underground* with C

that looked as if it had been crumbled and then kneaded by history itself. Up here on the high Anatolian plateau troglodytes had been tunnelling into the ground for millennia: there were meant to be whole cities constructed souterrain, in which the natives had waited out the depredations of whichever invading army – Greeks, Romans, Persians, Ottomans – happened to be marching through at the time. Perhaps, I mused, it was one such legion of transients, cleverly tricked into tramping along a handy fissure, whose ghosts were now perturbing the earth?

Central Turkey had the look of antiquity about it. Even the modern settlements had the appearance of rime, as if their substance had crystallised out of the crust they stood on. Yet as subsequent earthquakes in Ankara and along the shores of the Black Sea would so disastrously confirm, contemporary Turkey was a society whose urbanity was constructed out of dangerously substandard concrete; powdery, friable stuff, readily pulverised by the slightest shake. Personally, I blamed the oblong shape of the country. After Nepal, Turkey is the most oblong country I've ever visited, but a glance at any reasonably good map will soon tell you that oblong countries have a high incidence of natural disasters and usually fairly grim human rights records as well.

Chile, Israel, Togo, Portugal . . . this list is by no means exhaustive – or even fair – but when it comes to whacko theories there's no reason why psychogeographers can't get in on the act. Anyway, to get back to Cappadocia, it had been a gruelling day's drive. As we'd ascended the plateau from Konya in our rental Fiat, I'd begun to notice a peculiar, prismatic distortion beginning in my left eye, which then spread gradually to the right. It was as if some sadistic ocular surgeon had inserted a prism into my retina, which was refracting the harsh light into swirling, kaleidoscopic patterns. I couldn't bear to tell John about it, because he might insist on driving. I don't do passenger.

There was this, and there was also the knowledge that this wasn't the first time I'd experienced the distortion. In fact, it had happened a couple of times before when I'd been climbing Scottish mountains. I'd be fine up to 3,000 feet, and then bingo! my eyes would turn into children's toys. Within hours of my descent a kind of clarity would return. Sitting that night in the lobby of our troglodyte hotel, watching the earthshaking news from Bush House, it impinged on me that perhaps my eye problem was also an act of God. God wanted me to stay down, or even go lower; that way I wouldn't escape the retributive ruckling of his premier creation.

# Hitler in Rio

São Paulo was – to adopt an idiom – way too much. The ride in from the airport through asteroid belt of the *favelas*, and then the planetary scale of the urban mass itself. Sitting in a restaurant atop the highest building in the city, I could see what looked like a snaggle of teeth on the horizon some twenty miles away, but when I scrutinised them carefully I saw that they too were equally vast edifices. The comprehension gap was as disorienting as the culture shock. In my four-star hotel I couldn't find one staff member who spoke more than rudimentary English or French; if you wanted to get anywhere here you needed Portuguese or German.

I couldn't get my plastic to work in the cash machines, so one afternoon I set out to find a bank where I could draw some money. I walked and I walked. As well as being illimitable São Paulo seemed to have little or no comprehensible street plan. It was like an unholy miscegenation between London and Los Angeles: mighty metropolises, grey and golden and exhaust-stained, humping at the place of dead roads. In some dusty square, metal-tortured boulevard or another, I fell in with an elderly German who spoke sinisterly good English. I say sinisterly because everything about him was sinister to my paranoiac mind. What was he doing here? Why did he talk about himself so circumspectly, but want to know all about me? I could almost visualise the death's head badges of the SS on his faded Hawaiian shirt.

The minibar in the hotel was no help. It was called the Selfbar – so I took it personally and downed the lot: the scotches, the vodkas, the gins and the Amazonian armpit aguardientes. Then I howled down the lift shaft. My Brazilian translator, the redoubtable Hamilton dos Santos, seeing the state I was getting into, suggested a little R&R in Rio. I flew there on a Varig flight for which there was no internal security. This was ten years ago, and perhaps things have changed since, but in those days the explanation Brazilians gave me for the lack of metal detectors at their airports was that everyone insisted on packing guns.

RISE and FALL

It was drizzling in Rio when I arrived, and the scuzzy grey shanty towns on the surrounding peaks threatened to topple on to Copacabana. In place of the sparkling strand of my imagination – crowded with promenading, steatopygous lovelies, their café-au-lait buttocks cloven by itsy-bitsy G-strings – I found instead three men in anoraks fishing the angry Atlantic while seated on collapsible stools. Shit! I admonished myself; I need never have left East Finchley after all!

If São Paulo was threatening, Rio was terrifying, but I had nothing to read, which is the most frightening thing of all when abroad. I went out with my money in my sock to find an English-language bookshop and couldn't, anywhere. Eventually I discovered one a bus ride away at a shopping mall in an outer suburb. They had three shelves of airport dross and one copy of William L. Shirer's magisterial *The Rise and Fall of the Third Reich*. I snapped it up.

I spent the next week snuggled up to the tiny zinc-topped bar of the tiny café opposite my hotel, assiduously working my way through Shirer. In the scary atmosphere of Rio the horrors perpetrated by the Nazis seemed almost gemütlich. I'd also, sensibly, switched to beer. Gradually, day by day, I felt the chaotic life around me beginning to assume some kind of coherence. I noticed that the street urchins, the hawkers, the washerwomen, the service workers for the skyscraper hotels lining the beach – the whole population of this quarter in fact – all knew one another and looked out for each other. Every individual had its niche in the living reef, and if a new creature came into the area its character – and potential to be a threat – was instantly noted. Far from being a soulless adjunct to the dubious delights of Copacabana, in this, the off-season, I could appreciate the tightly knit community I found myself in.

On the final night I spent in Rio I broached the language barrier and fell in with a couple of good-time girls. I say 'girls' advisedly, because although they looked younger than me, such were the concertinaed demographics of Brazil that one of them turned out to be a grandmother. Anyway, by a combination of signs and pidgin English I managed to convey to these two the extent of my sociological observations of Copacabana. 'Oh yes,' Vittoria replied, 'we know everyone here, and if anyone new comes and we don't know their name, they get given a nickname so we can easily identify them.'

'So,' I asked, not a little incurious, 'have I got a nickname?'

'Of course!' She gestured at the prominent swastika on the cover of my Shirer. 'We call you Hitler.'

# A Handful
# of Carbohydrate

Two decades ago I spent three months in India. My companion was Turnbull St Asser, the last scion of a North Country dynasty of enormous antiquity (they came over with the Cro-Magnons), who had dedicated thirty generations to dissipation and dilettantism. Turnbull and I had been at the varsity together and we shared a taste for the finer – and fouler – things in life, although coming from East Finchley my dandyism had a curiously neo-Marxist tinge. Inevitably we quarrelled in Kathmandu, after I threw some coloured water on his Shantung silk suit during the festival of Holi. Turnbull departed to stay with some maharaja or another to whom he had a letter of introduction, while I headed by minibus for Varanasi (see 'The Holy City', page 83).

Strange though it may seem now, we arranged to rendezvous a month later at Srinagar, in Kashmir, to see if we could resolve our differences; ah, such is the folly of youth! After an unscheduled extra week on the banks of the sacred Ganga, I entrained and took the thundering Himigiri–Howrah Express across the north of the subcontinent to Chandigarh. On the train, slotted into a third-class couchette like a beige filing cabinet drawer, I met a young couple from Maidstone. We discussed life, love, politics, religion and the future of mankind. I wrote some jejune verses in the girl's commonplace book. When we parted I breathed a sigh of relief.

Fifteen years later she pitched up again while I was signing books at Hatchards in Piccadilly, and, yes, she had the jejune verses. Truly, notoriety is a depth charge to your acquaintance, throwing up all sorts of dead fish, and for that reason alone it is to be avoided.

There was no avoiding Turnbull either. At the appointed hour I arrived at the Tourist Office and sat huddled on a stone bench. It was cold in Kashmir, especially so after the heat of the plains. The locals went around with portable charcoal stoves, which they sat with underneath their djellabas. It looked right toasty to me, who was clad in regulation travellers' denims, set off with bits of embroidered cotton wrapped around my extremities. 'My God!' expostulated Turnbull, striding towards me, his tweeds whispering affluently, 'you've gone bloody native!'

Turnbull, however, had already paid for his cultural arrogance. With his flame of hair and flashing monocle, the impoverished houseboat proprietors had seen him coming rather better than he was able to descry them. In 1984 Kashmir was yet to descend into the war of insurgency that has since devastated the region, but the Indian army was there in strength, and the tension was driving away the tourists. Out on Dal Lake the flotillas of houseboats, with their ornate, fretworked superstructures, were mostly empty. There was hardly anyone about to be taken to the famous floating gardens. Knockdown deals were the order of the day: for $2 a day I was staying on the Houseboat Ceylon, with full board, laundry services and excursion transport thrown in, courtesy of its efficient proprietor, Rashid.

Turnbull, on the other hand, was paying twenty bucks a night for a stinky berth on a muddy barge moored in a sewer running off the Jhelum River. No food, no transport, and certainly no dry-cleaning for his suits. I laughed long and loud when I saw his quarters: 'Ho, ho, ho, ho, ho!' I went, hoping to pay back in some small measure the centuries of Schadenfreude the St Assers had exacted from their tenants, 'You've been rooked!'

An hour later Turnbull was ensconced with me on the HB Ceylon and we had begun to bicker all over again. Rashid, hating dissension of any kind, suggested we take a trip into the Himalaya; he would organise everything. He was as good as his word, and two days later we were clopping up into the terrifying Pir Panjal Range, Turnbull and I mounted on laden donkeys, while Rashid took the lead on foot. Turnbull looked ridiculous in a blanket he contrived to wear like a Mexican poncho, and a pearl-grey fedora. I was still cold.

When we reached our destination, a mountain hut at 15,000 feet that looked like a cricket pavilion, I was a hell of a lot colder. We were there for two days but it felt like two weeks. Rashid fed us indigestible meals of bread, rice and potatoes. 'Carbohydrate, carbohydrate, carbohydrate!' Turnbull admonished him, 'that's three kinds of carbohydrate!' We took to our sleeping bags, and Turnbull then tormented me by reading aloud lengthy descriptions of princely feasting in a book he'd borrowed from his maharaja: 'Twenty-eight capons stuffed with sweet almonds, a pie of larks' tongues and live song birds, jellied crocodile kidneys . . .' – on and on he brayed. In many ways I feel I've never left that hideous place, and that my whole life has been spent in a high-altitude cricket pavilion being persecuted by an English aristo. But at least I know I'm not alone.

127

TILTING AT WILLMILLS

# Thai Strip

In Thailand the sybaritic life on a farang-only island off Phuket was about as appealing to me as a shit-smelling durian. The pink Western porkers were massaged by little brown Thais and served up with that worldwide luxury hotel fare which always involves American pancakes and sculpted melons.

Bangkok felt better; a lot better. Men carried grandfather clocks through the flooded streets, streams of tuk-tuks farted out noxious fumes – two strokes and you're out. Along every side alley were food stalls offering sizzling snacks. You could graze your way from one temple to the next giant Buddha, being alternately steeped in chilli and the polymorphous perversity of Thai religious iconography. We found a reasonable, family-run guesthouse in the outer northern suburb of Nonthaburi. There were the usual Kiwis playing Boggle, a bespectacled German living out some von Aschenbach fantasy and our landlady, Mrs Rai, who together with her family wove their lives into those of their guests. I chucked a baseball back and forth with her pubescent son, and checked English homework with her daughter.

The garden of the house ran nearly down to the river, and a few minutes' walk away was a khlong where we could catch the longtail boats into the city centre. The longtails were really the best thing about the city for the visitor – high-prowed vessels powered by enormous outboard engines that sent up great frothy washes as they parted the brown waters of the Chao Phraya at a rate of knots. To ride them, along with two score salarymen and women, was to share vicariously in the frenetic pulse of the working city. Still, no matter how we strived, the sheer scale and hub-bub of Bangkok was exhausting, and the afternoon heat usually saw us poleaxed in our room, under the fan, blearying at the curious spectacle of an entire wall given over to a giant poster of the Manhattan skyline at night.

Manhattan is the most iconic of cities, true, but, still, I'd rather have had a wall-sized poster of the skyline of Bangkok; that at least would've made me feel I'd arrived. But it wasn't the most obtrusive Manhattan skyline I've ever shared a transient's room with. That dubious distinction belongs to the Hotel Britannia in Manchester. Here, in the very humming core of the four-square building, with its cavernous bars full of superannuated soap actors, and its hypogean discotheque (called something like Hades or the Ninth Circle), I found myself tenanting a room without windows.

To check into a hotel room without windows once is just about a bearable novelty, even if that room has one wall taken up with red curtains, which, when swished aside, revealed a sinisterly top-lit, wall-sized poster of the skyline of Manhattan. I bedded down for the night and in the small hours was afflicted with the most terrible dreams of being buried alive. Gagging on consciousness I snapped on the bedside light, and, not remembering where I was, lunged for the curtains, only to be confronted by the dark outlines of the Chrysler Building, the Empire State, et al.

It was a truly sublime moment, as I reeled back in awe at the sight of this. Was I perhaps in New York? I poked at the vision and its paper surface yielded slightly. No, New York seemed unlikely; after all, what creepy mind-warper of an hotelier would cover a real view with a fake one? In that case, was I back at Mrs Rai's in Nonthaburi? My Thai trip had been eight years previously, and yet stranger holes in the space-time continuum have been breached. It took me a good few minutes of examining phone pads and checking my own belongings to resolve this disorientation, and then I swore never to be put in the windowless Manhattan suite ever again.

But the Big Apple can never be wholly cored, and it crops up in the most inapposite places. Why, for instance, is there a large photograph of the booking hall at Grand Central Station on the wall of the cafeteria in my local Sainsbury's? Supping weak tea and eating sloppy lasagne, are us customers meant to reflect on the umbilical linkage between Vauxhall in south London and this temple to the railway age? I put this despairing question to Peter, a fellow psychogeographer, and he blanched, while a snail trail of sweat wormed its way down from his sparse hairline. 'It's strange you should say that,' he replied in a faint voice, 'but I'd just bought a ticket for Poughkeepsie the other week, and was on my way to track 129 from the booking hall, when I found this on the stairs.' He produced a dog-eared Polaroid of the cafeteria at the Nine Elms Sainsbury's.

It was proof, as if any were needed, that the world – as anyone who's travelled it can tell you – is not a globe but a Möbius strip.

MANHATTAN GRAND CENTRAL PARK SUMMER PALACE, BAN

K VISHNU VEHICLE GARUDA AS HOTEL WALLPAPER. Ralph STEADman 2004

# Modelling the Neapolitan

In 2000 I was hired by the film director Bernardo Bertolucci to write a short story based on a film script he already had. The action was set in Naples, partly during the Renaissance and partly in the contemporary city. If he liked it, he was then going to get someone else to turn it back into another film script. I know this sounds like a roundabout way of arriving at a film, but the movie business is a strange one in which creative properties undergo preposterous metamorphoses: TV adverts are made into films, so are computer games; for all I know some tyro producer is currently developing a film based on a supermarket's ready meal.

I visited Naples for four days to sop up the atmosphere and found the city cavernous, threatening and deathly. Almost the entire population had cleared out to Ischia, the Amalfi Coast and Capri, because it was the Eve of the Assumption in mid-August. I wished I'd been there for the Festival of San Gennaro, the city's patron saint. A vial, purportedly containing this personage's dried blood, is kept in the cathedral; and twice a year, on appointed days, it liquefies. Or not. Liquefaction years are good ones, full of prosperity and joy; dry years are bad ones: the football team loses, the volcano erupts, Berlusconi remains in power.

Perhaps the greatest book on the city by an outsider is Norman Lewis's *Naples '44*, his account of a year spent in the Neapolitan labyrinth as a British Army intelligence officer (although, as he sagely remarks at the outset, 'military intelligence' is an almost perfect oxymoron). Lewis was treated to all sorts of wondrous occurrences, and his memoir conjures up vividly a society in which natural magic was still as potent as technology. The year before he arrived Padre Pio, the miraculous monk, had regularly been sighted flying like a cassock-clad Superman over Vesuvius, and plucking plummeting Italian airmen out of the sky.

My own, brief sojourn in this astonishing encrustation of urbanity – the impasto of successive architectural eras, Hellenistic, Roman, Medieval, Renaissance, is so thick as to be geologic – was distinctly downbeat in comparison. I put up in a modern hotel on the Partenope, a sea-front strand facing the dell'Ovo Castle, and made forays into the old town. Starting at Gambrinus, the exuberant art nouveau café on the expansive Piazza Reale, I gave it a good crack, gothicking along with the best of them. I visited this church, that cloister, the other convent. I plunged into crypts and stroked petrified catafalques – an act which can have you arrested anywhere but Naples. I stopped at a restaurant and, directed by the waiter, ate a selection of local delicacies, most of which – to be frank – looked and tasted like Ambrosia creamed rice. Yummy.

I walked over to the scuzzy part of town, between the port and the station, where Naples's renowned transvestites ply their silicone wares, and Somalians with golf-ball heads and golf-club bodies do strange things with cloned Samsonite luggage. I rode on the subway – amazingly, it was even more minatory than the narrow alley-ways of the old town. I visited an estate agent and discovered that if I wanted to move to Naples I could buy most of a sixteenth-century palazzo for half the price of my London gaff. I took the funicular up the steep hill to the Castel Sant'Elmo and wandered the battlements, looking out over the Ribena-dark sea. At night, I went along to the Villa Communale, a dusty strip of park on the seashore, where there were free concerts of Neapolitan music. To my tin ear and jaundiced eye, these seemed like exceedingly well-groomed dogs howling at the bloody full moon of high summer.

In short, I did what I could, and yet Naples utterly eluded me. It was too dense, too impacted, too other, too rich in meaning, and I wasn't there for 1/100th of the necessary time. The only things I found at all comprehensible were the *presepe*. These were curious models of idealised scenes – part rustic, part sacerdotal – enacted against backdrops of ruined classical architecture. Most Neapolitan churches have a *presepe* and a lot of private homes as well. In their glass cases they encapsulate the entire spirit of the place 'sacrificing the sensible', as Lévi-Strauss puts it, 'in favour of the intelligible'.

In Naples there's an entire street devoted to *presepe*, little shops with baskets in front of them full of thousands of cherubs, angels, infant Jesuses, saints, demons, Mary Magdalenes, shepherds, &c. As well as the figures you can get the neces-sary ivy-choked columns and collapsed mangers to place them among. The *presepe* are so integral to Naples, with their peculiar air of being part magical juju, part baroque decoration, that someone should really make a film based on them.

# Bend Sinister

To the City for the annual Doggett's Coat and Badge Race. Taking place at the end of July every year since the early eighteenth century, it is the oldest annually contested event in the British sporting calendar. It's a rowing race for single sculls, and the course is four and a half miles from London Bridge, against the ebb tide, to Cadogan Pier in Chelsea.

Doggett himself was a comedian and manager of Drury Lane Theatre, but since his death the race has been under the auspices of the Fishmongers' Company. My friend Julian is a Fishmonger and had extended me an invitation to view the race from the Company's hired boat, followed by a slap-up lunch in their opulent Hall. Of course, he isn't literally a fishmonger (I don't believe he even likes fish), because this is a City Livery Company, and while the Fishmongers' retains more links with the trade than, say, the Goldsmiths', it is in essence a living fossil; a medieval guild, cemented to the Square Mile like an oyster, through which flows a great current of nutritious pelf.

I suited up, entrained to Bank and then walked down through the back streets to Swan Lane Pier. The City of London is a bit of a nightmare for the psychogeographer; two thousand years of human interaction have worked over this tiny allotment of earth with savage intensity, digging into it, raising it up and covering over the very watercourses. Now, as one of the three global financial centres, the poisoned air of the place ultrasonically whines with the electronic transmission of trillions, while sweaty-shirted clerks suck filter tips beneath the hard haunches of its institutions. Standing under a spreading chestnut tree in Suffolk Lane, just off Cannon Street, I stared into the immaculate interior of a vacant office suite which had been sculpted out of a Queen Anne town house. Its off-white wainscotting was unleant upon, its beige cabling unused. The thought of how much money was represented by these thousand-odd square feet lying idle made my head spin. I walked on.

At the river the boat was loading up with Fishmongers, their wives and children.

We were ushered on board by a previous winner of the race, a wizened boy wearing an antique suit of scarlet. The four oarsmen who were to contest this year's race were already alongside. So low were the decks of their rapier-like sculls that they appeared to be sitting in the choppy water of the Thames, with its sinisterly beautiful bloom of subsurface silt. The Prime Warden's launch appeared; on board was the Barge Master, wearing a cockade hat and a frogged coat with an epaulette on its right shoulder like a gold platter.

Loudhailers crackled out Cockney information: 'If yer wanta know anyfing abaht ve oarsmen, ask ve steward an' eel tell ya.' Race slips were passed among the champers-supping mongers, the sunlight danced on the water. Sitting here, in the very cockpit of ultra-urbanity, with a scale replica of the Golden Hind moored in the notch of St Katharine's Dock across the river, and the high stony mundanity of London Bridge soaring overhead, I felt the dangerous tickle of full temporal simultaneity agitate my psyche. Then they were off, rowing hard against the tide.

It's a measure of the awesome power of this plutocratic oligopoly that all traffic on the river was stopped for the forty-minute duration of the race. In splendid isolation our flotilla proceeded upstream past central London's burnished landmarks. 'The race,' Julian remarked knowledgeably, 'is effectively decided in the first few minutes.' And that much was clear; holding the crown of the river, the oarsman in the yellow singlet had immediately pulled ahead, leaving the other competitors floundering. One made for the inside of the bend, past the culture reef of the South Bank Centre; another disappeared behind a refuse barge moored in midstream; the third was so far back that I feared he might be mowed down by our boat, and all this for a red suit and a silver badge representing 'Liberty'.

Well, not exactly. The truth is that, like any City ritual, the Doggett's Coat and Badge Race represents a theatrical performance of a political reality. By commandeering four miles of the river, the Fishmongers cast the reticulation of their power over its sinuous coils, netting in the process many silvery shoals. Back at their Hall, a four-square edifice on the end of London Bridge rebuilt three times in the past millennium, scallops, monkfish and prawns were ingested by me, while Julian had the chicken. We wandered through the luxuriously appointed chambers to see the exhibit which holds pride of place: the dagger with which Sir William Walworth, the then Lord Mayor of London, stabbed to death Wat Tyler under the very eyes of Richard II, thus breaking the Peasants' Revolt and – arguably – setting back the cause of democracy in Britain by three hundred years.

The dagger appears sinisterly well made and beautifully sharp, as befits a
Fishmongers' knife.

# Sizewell Again

Sizewell again. This patch of Suffolk coastline, psychically irradiated by the untold ergs of electricity generated by the two nuclear power stations, exerts a strange hold on me. I far prefer it to the environs of Southwold, further up the coast, which have become overwritten by scribes as various as P.D. James and W.G. Sebald. I lived inland of here for a couple of years in the mid-1990s but was forced to evacuate when the wife of the one local acquaintance I'd made invited me to 'drop by' her gift shop when I was next in Saxmundham. I was on the phone to the self-drive van hire company that very evening.

The two power stations – 'A', a humungous, four-square chunk of 1960s concrete, complete with outsize transom windows; 'B', a 1980s plinth of dark, yet iridescent blue steel, topped off by a vast golf ball of a dome – squat in back of the dunes, willing you to impose your own imaginative vision on them. I think the Supreme Ruler of the Entire Known Universe will probably take a lease on 'B' some time in the future, furnishing it with 100-metre-long smoked glass coffee tables and square hectares of quarry tiling. 'A' will become a charmingly recherché guest annexe.

The interzone between the fortified plutonium piles and the sea has been landscaped since I was last here, dinky hillocks skilfully mounded by British Nuclear Fuels, then planted with reed, furze and alien-flesh samphire. But offshore the two iron platforms which mark the intake and outflow of the power stations' cooling system remain, streaked with rust and guano, capped by wheeling gulls. This plot of water is a few degrees warmer than the surrounding North Sea, so it attracts fish, fowl and fishermen, links in a strange food chain. The fishermen come mostly from the Midlands. Having headed in large numbers due east across country, as if summoned by some collective, phylogenetic impulse, they erect their little nylon huts on the beach. Here they sit until dawn, dabbling their lines in the Roentgen briny, sucking on filter tips and cans of Stella Artois, a peculiar temporary settlement of moody anchorites.

The beach has a visitor car park and a prefab tea shop dubbed, appropriately enough, Sizewell 'T'; while drawn up on the shingle is the fag end of a centuries-old inshore fishing fleet, clinker-built and tar-caulked; but neither industry nor

leisure can truly impose itself on Sizewell, where the collision between crumbling coastline and a human artefact with a guaranteed lethal half-life of tens of thousands of years induces a sense of exhilarating queasiness: deep time interpenetrating every grain of sand.

The small boys demanded an isolated camping spot, so their mother and I

hauled our mishmash of equipment out along the beach, to where the BNFL land marches with the Minsmere Nature Reserve. Here, in a thicket of dwarf oaks, we erected our two-person tent. The campsite was soon invaded by many tens of hover flies, attracted by the gaudy flysheet. These curiously attractive insects looked like smallish bees redesigned by a contemporary jeweller: their flattened, angular abdomens had jagged markings, their compound eyes a grey sheen. Later, when we hit the beach, we found a positive wrack of them, lying dead above the tide line.

Darkness fell and the obligatory sausages were eaten, then it was back to the beach for a bonfire. The Matriarch pulled this off in fine style, arranging driftwood against a half-buried concrete dragon's tooth with an artistry that would've caused Richard Long to tear his own heart out with envy and throw it, still beating, to the ground. The oily spars burnt green and purple, the slack waves rattled the shingle; we were snug in a little sitting room carved out of the soft night.

The following afternoon, heading back to the Great Wen, I turned the car off the road on to a track. I wanted to see a house that I remembered from ten years before. A perfectly nice dyad of farm labourers' cottages, remarkable only in that they are tucked up in a dell within a hundred metres of the fizzing, popping hank of power lines that loop from the power stations to the first of the pylons, then march, seriatim, across the flat lands in the direction of Ipswich.

A decade before the house was untenanted, and it was difficult to imagine who would want to reside in this potential cancer risk; but now there was a young, well-spoken man, tinkering with an immaculate vintage motorcycle in the garage. We chatted a bit, and he laughingly acknowledged the preposterous character of the dwelling. Our six-year-old, sensing a toehold, chimed up from the back seat: 'Excuse me, when we come back here again, can we visit your house properly?' Sizewell, again.

# Bouncy Metropolis

In the early medieval period the lives of countless peasants were defined by their relation to the castle. From the stern keep of the Norman overlord issued forth decrees and exactions; in a world of wood, wheat and water, its high stone walls were the most adamantine confirmation of the temporal order, just as the acuminate spire of the church pricked the oppressive heavens. Writing, then, as a descendant of peasants, it seems only meet that I should testify to the manner in which my own life has revolved around and been shaped by the lineal descendant of these bastions. I refer, of course, to the bouncy castle.

I first went on a bouncy castle in the early 1960s. It was a wholly enclosed, striped, latex structure positioned on Brighton's West Pier. Moon-walking around its interior, which whined with the ultrasonic echoes of other screeching children, I felt oddly empowered, ready to leap in my stockinged feet through some mystic portal and into the very future itself. How right I was. It seems to me that, throughout the seventies, eighties and nineties as the influence of Windsor Castle has waned so that of the bouncy castle has waxed. Could the two phenomena by any chance be related? After all, it's impossible to retain any faith in the monarchical principle if you've grown up leaping around on a rubber simulacrum of their hallowed halls.

In 1980 I got a vacation job for the old Greater London Council's Recreation Department. Together with a handful of other bohemian types I was responsible for the 'inflatable project'. This involved constructing freeform inflatable structures and then transporting them around London parks during the school holidays. In charge of the inflatables was James, a one-time organiser – together with Brian Eno – of the Portsmouth Sinfonia. This avant-garde ensemble comprised scores of unlearned instrumentalists who would gather together to hack spontaneously – and unmercifully – away at classical music standards. The Sinfonia had a

top thirty hit in September of 1981 with their 'Classical Muddly' – I was much impressed.

James, who also tutored at the Slade, brought a certain brio to the construction of bouncy castles. There was 'the Child Psychologist's Nightmare', a bizarre maze of black and red tubes; 'the Big H', which was just that; and there were assorted giant spheres and rhomboids which we, the soi-disant 'playleaders', could climb inside and be pushed about by hundreds of squealing kids. I tell you it was a fine sight when all the blowers were working properly and some urban veldt was scattered with these Pantagruelian playthings. We would get anything up to five hundred kids a session, supervised by just four adults; and often, when ten or so sprogs leapt on to the crosspiece of the 'H', another forty would be thrown high into the air off its uprights. None of the structures was enclosed and yet injuries were far from common.

In those days the GLC had suzerainty over a number of open spaces unincorporated by the London boroughs. These were scattered as far afield as Thamesmead in the east, Eltham in the deep south, Shepherd's Bush in the west and Alexandra Park in the north. So it was that I came to an adult consciousness of the geography of my natal city through the praxis of bouncy castles. For me London is neither the moneyed bulk of the City nor the bright lights of the West End; rather, it is an endless realm of boating lakes, bowling greens, football pitches and adventure playgrounds, all scarified by the summer heat and populated by a strange race of yammering gnomes, their faces coated with sucrose.

The second summer I worked on the inflatables we were joined by Phil, and he and I split off into a subsidiary team. Phil had a strange phobia about driving through tunnels which had something to do with a coach trip and LSD. Needless to say, cruelly, we tricked him into driving the van full of inflatables through the Rotherhithe Tunnel. We all survived, but years later Phil has become an academic specialising in contemporary British fiction. I blame myself.

When Ken Livingstone returned to power in London I felt certain that he'd resurrect the inflatables project; after all, what could be more suited to modern London, with its ludicrous insubstantiality? I waited and waited for the call to come from the mayoralty but to no avail. Then, walking along the Embankment, the reason struck why they hadn't rung. Far from being a thing of the past, the inflatables had now been fully incorporated into the London skyline: the Gherkin, the Greater London Assembly, countless other new buildings throughout the city, all have a curvilinear form suggestive of inflated latex. No wonder we walk with a wholly unjustified bounce in our step – we're living in a bouncy metropolis.

# Back to
# the Renaissance

I'll go a long way for a good display of birds of prey – even Tuscany if required. Filing into the Palazzo Pubblico in Siena we encountered two arrant narcissists all done up in high leather boots, tight tan jodhpurs and voluminous white blouses. Granted, they had the aquiline good looks and slinky hips needed to carry off this rig, and they also had the correct avian accessories: the young woman a goshawk, the young man an eagle owl. These raptors were poised elegantly on the narcissists' leather gauntlets, their luminous yellow eyes unblinking in the bright light of the Piazza del Campo, an expression of cruel disdain for all tourists on their feathery faces. I took the proffered leaflet and shuffled on in.

After a profitable half-hour or so limning in the significance of Ambrogio Lorenzetti's masterpiece *Effects of Good and Bad Government* for my six-year-old (and, in fairness to him, he had a better grasp on the allegory than I did), we tumbled out of the finest example of fourteenth-century vernacular architecture in the known world and went in search of the birdy leather fetishists. Across the Piazza del Mercato we strolled, then dropped down through the city walls into one of the 'basins' which nestle between the spurs of Siena's red hills.

Within a few metres everything had gone leafy and we were passing by authentic Sienese allotments, full of runner beans, flowering peas and pendulous tomatoes. Ranged along benches which bordered a small field at the bottom of the hill, we could see an assembly of international bourgeoisie gathered for the display. In the middle of the field the fashion-plate falconers were pirouetting and striking attitudes.

Now, a good bird of prey display can be a magnificent thing. Talked by an expert into the Weltanschauung of a high-soaring, speedy-swooping hawk, which can read a newspaper headline at a distance of a mile (which explains why you never see a raptor actually buy a newspaper), the suggestible punter feels himself to be at one with the bird. I fondly imagined that here in the very embrace of this

most beautiful of Renaissance cities, the metamorphosis would be easily effected, and I would find myself whipping through the slipstream above the zebra-striped Duomo, my arms tawny and tessellated.

Over the course of raising two sons with raptor obsessions I've attended a great many birds of prey displays and become something of an aficionado. I have to say that, while there's a certain frisson to be gained from the display at London Zoo, where a high-kicking secretary bird despatches a rubber snake with its barbed tootsies, my absolute favourite has to be the magnificent show put on at the Hawk Conservancy in Hampshire. This stars a brace of bald eagles, which loop out over the counterpane landscape for miles before returning, unerringly, to their handler's mitt.

In my current ranking of such divertissements, I can – with some mean glee – assure you that the Sienese example came bottom. This was the worst birds of prey display it was possible to imagine; indeed, it was only saved from being a complete disaster by going badly wrong. I'll explain. Albinoni tootled and rasped from a couple of speakers, a commanding and patriarchal narcissist (his blouse more voluminous, his hair iron-grey) strode on to the dusty sward. 'I don't like your big boots,' sneered Luther (aged three). It was an inauspicious opening.

The Albinoni cut out, and using a hand mic' the falconer gave us the usual spiel: history of hawking, capabilities of birds, &c. Then he took delivery of a goshawk from his lovely assistant and launched it into the sparkling air. The bird rapidly gained height towards the church of Santa Maria dei Servi, then disappeared. The falconer tried whirling his lure but to no avail – the bird had flown. He had only one possible course of action: loose a second hawk. This was done with some expeditiousness. Once again the bird mounted towards the skyline – and disappeared.

The falconer chirred and whooped, ululated and yelped. He put on such a performance that, far from being transported with the birds, I was left severely benchbound and regretting my 19 euro expenditure. Then, finally, one of the hawks came barrelling back down. The falconer, caught unawares, had the lure grabbed from his hand and suddenly there was one freaked-out bird flapping about within feet of us, trying to choke down its meaty reward. But before we could take this spectacle on board, the second hawk came whirring over our heads and savagely attacked the first. Next the falconers piled in – all three of them – and their tan-clad legs tangled with jesses, talons and beating wings, then the ghoulish spectators flocked to this perverse photo opportunity.

There is, of course, a lesson in all of this. When you find yourself in a touristic situation don't try and buck the trend. We were meant to be looking at the Renaissance – not having our eyes pecked out by it.

# The Sound
# of the Suburbs

Footlocker in Brixton on a Saturday afternoon. The ordered civility I remember from my own childhood, when Start-rite sandals were fitted by mock-obsequious girls in 'shk-shk' nylon, has given way to this curious free-for-all. Four or five video screens dangle from the dark ceiling of the shop, and four or five Britney Spears jiggle and jive and gurn. Assistants in the black-and-white, vertically striped shirts of American basketball referees seem to accost customers at random. On the walls are rack upon rack of hybridised training shoes. The training shoe as combat boot, ballet slipper, jackboot, wheelless sports car, alien appendage – is there any limit to the versatility of this footwear, which must have been responsible for the flattening of the feet of billions?

I could get stressed. The little boys have run amok, they've tied their Action Men on to lengths of string and are whirling them about their ears. My eldest – at fourteen emphatically too old to be out Saturday shopping with his dad – lounges over by the clothes rails. Doubtless in his fervid mind he is running a string of bootylicious hos in the 'hood. That leaves me and my daughter, struggling to find the right chunk of rubber and leather in the right size. At last we achieve this, and, freshly shod, debouch into the sunlight, where Mormon missionaries and the Nation of Islam do battle for the souls of the teeming crowd.

A major dérive is in order; we have to be yanked out of all this intense urbanity – only the 'burbs have the requisite balm. The five of us entrain from Brixton Station, and within half an hour we're in Petts Wood, a planned interwar garden suburb, heavily Arts and Crafts influenced, two miles from Orpington. Almost instantly I feel myself relaxing, the tension courses from my shoulders, flows across the pavement and enters those of my eldest son. Christ! How he hates the suburbs – I can see the distaste etched all over his face. I know what he feels like, how the red brick, the pantiles, the stained-glass fanlights are all bearing down on him

SUBURBANAL

Ralph STEADman 2004

153

– because I felt exactly the same way at his age, as if I was about to be suffocated by the sheer orderliness of all the neat verges and linseed-oiled garage doors. Just to make him feel worse, I offer to rent a house for him and his mates so they can debauch together. There's only one catch – it has to be in Petts Wood.

We stroll on and into the wood itself, a substantial chunk of primordial woodland left immured by London. Sessile oak, beech and silver birch crowd around the sandy track, the sunlight twinkles from between the interlocking boughs, the little boys cavort, the adolescents even begin to frolic a bit. Two miles brings us to the remains of Scadbury Manor, a medieval moated house. It's been excavated and the tall brick chimneypieces and barrel-vaulted cellars are exposed to view. In the weed-choked moat some coots do their thing. We stand looking south through the fringing trees, to where the Swanley interchange of the M25 grumbles in the mid-distance.

I am ridiculously happy. I love these interzones, where country and city do battle for the soul of a place. I can sense the last few roads of semis below us in the valley, and beyond them the open fields. We're only a few miles from the village of Downe, where Charles Darwin lived out his years selectively breeding pigeons. I like to think he would've appreciated this dérive as a sound survival mechanism, the only possible way to stay mentally fit in the psychotic entrails of a twenty-first century megalopolis. Then we walk on to Sidcup through cluttered, darkling fields.

Sidcup is one of those outer London suburbs that have achieved the sublime status of place-name-as-insult. Pinter made much of the place in *The Caretaker*, the trampish protagonist of which is forever on his way to Sidcup to 'get me papers'. But we don't get to see much of the place; night is falling on the valley of the River Cray as we limp into the town centre. There's time for burgers and kebabs in a Turkish-run chippie, before we proceed to the station and entrain for London Bridge.

On the train are Sidcup lads and lasses glammed up for a Saturday night up in the Smoke. I lean over to my eldest: 'See that chap over there,' I whisper, 'we're so far out in the sticks he's unashamedly sporting a mullet!' My son winces. But then, as the train clatters over the great silvery river of tracks which are being fed into London Bridge, I can see the tension seep out of his shoulders. He's safe, back in the warm beating heart of his natal city. I, on the other hand, feel dreadful again.

# Right to
# Urban Roaming

I welcome the new right to roam, yes indeedy I do. After all, I'm a committed walker with the yards of nylon and feet of Gore-Tex to prove it. There's nothing I like more than a good walk and most mornings I begin the day with a little hike to the bathroom, where I choke down a bit of Kendal Mint Cake while liberally pissing. Then I walk downstairs to the kitchen, where I stop for a well-earned breakfast, usually a cereal bar broken up in a bowl with milk added. I call this concoction of my own devising 'muesli'. Then I walk back upstairs to my office. That's three walks even before I've started work!

I know lots of other people are keen on walking as well, because when I go out into the street I see them doing it, and if I head over to my local shop I often find Mike, the proprietor, plodding up and down the aisles of biscuits and Brillo pads. As we pass each other we'll sing out a cheery 'hello!' because we're just two walkers doing what we love and this engenders a certain fellow feeling. Many serious walkers are pretty down on the whole business of shopping, and see trolling around expensive retail outlets racking up consumer debt as a poor substitute for the windswept romance of the fells, but I say fie on you! On a good hike in the West End or around one of London's many indoor malls, I can travel as far as a mile, while the frequent stops to heave my plastic give the whole experience great style and elan.

I suppose the real objection to all this walking I do is that it takes the form of what's termed 'linear access'. I start at point 'A' and, using a direct route, walk to point 'B'. Granted, I may make diversions to points 'C' and 'D', but these too will be along fairly defined paths. What I don't do is 'roam', and that's precisely what the new Countryside and Rights of Way Act allows me to do. Personally, I find the whole notion of roaming quite alien, and I'm not even sure that I know how to do it at all. Take my morning routine: where am I to go if I don't walk to

the bathroom? Should I just stroll aimlessly around the bedroom until I end up pissing in the bookcase? This has been known to happen, but usually only after the ingestion of strong liquors. And what about my walk over the road to buy the paper? If I roam up and down Mike's aisles for too long, tolerant as he is he'll call the Old Bill.

I'm not just being facetious about this. As I say, I welcome the opening up of an area the size of Luxembourg to the British public, and concur heartily with those who say that for far too long the big landowners have been allowed to hide their bushels under a . . . er . . . bushel. But roaming, I ask you. I don't think we're going to see the Forest of Bowland – one of the new areas of outstanding natural beauty which has been opened up – covered with cagoule-clad worthies ambling about in a completely random pattern, like smoke particles in Brownian motion. Isn't it more likely that they'll naturally fuse into flocks and packs that will then denude the patches they settle on, and perhaps end up having to be painlessly culled by high-velocity rifle bullets?

Isn't the sordid truth that by turning walking, that most primal of physical activities, into a recreational pursuit like paragliding or motocross, the roaming lobby – quite inadvertently – participate in the downgrading of more workaday ambulatory activity? The kind of walking they have in mind requires a fair outlay on kit and usually – for those of us who live in large conurbations – a long train or car ride before it can be undertaken. Besides, isn't it the case that there can be no rights without responsibilities? And I'm not talking about shutting the gate here. The harsh fact is that far from taking responsibility for their walking the vast bulk of the population is more prepared than ever to sit around on its fat arses licking pure salt and watching reality TV shows.

Still, at least that leaves us linear walkers with plenty of elbow room. I walked to Newhaven this summer from the front door of my house in south London. It was eighty-seven miles and it took me four days. In the first three days out I encountered more people in electric invalid carriages (three) than I did on foot. On the fourth day this changed, because I'd got to the South Downs, which were covered with people roaming. It's an irony that can't be lost on the Duke of Westminster and his buddies, that, having lost unlimited grazing for one kind of livestock, they've now acquired another species.

# Havana
# . . . in Brighton

I went to a wedding at the weekend in Havana . . . in Brighton. Let us just dwell on that phrase for a few moments: I went to a wedding at the weekend in Havana . . . in Brighton. Havana was very nice as it happens, two large airy rooms, with galleries running around them, fans revolving lazily on the white-painted ceilings. The staff were bustling and efficient, wound tightly into their immaculate, ankle-length aprons. There was no sign either of the sleaze and corruption one associates with the Batista regime, or of the penury and paranoia that has dogged Fidel Castro's exercise in nation building. But then this was Havana . . . in Brighton.

I think it was brave of the bride and groom to hold their wedding in Havana, because the bride comes from an Anglo-Chinese family and they must have fairly negative feelings about communism. As for the groom, well, he's a dyed-in-the-cashmere capitalist, a true getter, so the venue must have seemed more than a tad outré. Still, he betrayed no anxiety as he ushered the guests in. There were painted ladies on stilts, a brace of conjurors, the food was noisettes of lamb, rosti, rugula salad – not quite what you expect from Cuban cuisine, but then this was Havana . . . in Brighton.

Later, as the Victoria train made a lengthy detour via Haywards Heath due to engineering works on the main line, I reflected on how Graham Greene might have reacted to the wedding. It's almost impossible to conceive of Greene visiting any kind of theme restaurant, even one as discreet as Havana. Perhaps this alone confirms that he wasn't quite the towering genius some once thought, and also explains why his books are beginning, ever so gently, to slide out of print. It seems to me incontrovertible that nothing that is human can be strange to those creators whose works will endure, not even an Irish pub in Maputo.

Had Havana been Brighton in the 1930s it would've allowed Greene to kill two fictional birds with one stone. He could've written a novel called *Our Man in*

*Havana Rocks . . . in Brighton*, the action of which would concern the sad machinations of a down-at-heel British spy running a theme restaurant who is threatened by a punk gangster. If you think this is preposterous, you need to consider the fact that Greene himself never even visited Brighton. During the composition of Brighton Rock he put up at the rather more genteel Bexhill-on-Sea and sent researchers along the coast to do his legwork for him.

I don't know why I've got it in for Greene at the moment – he never did anything to hurt me. Still, the revelation that, far from being an urbane globetrotter, he never got further than Sussex, while the vast bulk of his output was written in the vicinity of Clapham Common, is one I must share. It was not by accident that critics dubbed his late-colonial milieu, with its dipsomaniac expats, tormented priests and nymphomaniac natives 'Greeneland', because it was first and foremost a country of the mind. *The Human Factor, The Heart of the Matter, The Quiet American* – all of them were drummed up by a fantasist who knew no more of South America, Africa or South-East Asia than a schoolboy armed with a decent atlas. *Travels with my Aunt* should really have been entitled *Hanging Out with My Aunt*, while Greene's very first fiction, *Stamboul Train*, is a blatant lie, as any close reading of the text makes it perfectly clear that the train in question is travelling on the branch line from Ely to Peterborough.

Does it matter? I hear you ask. Surely it's a very prosaic conception of fiction indeed which insists on such a factual basis? After all, even Kafka wrote a novel called Amerika without ever going there. Well, yes and yet no. I do think a sense of topography is integral to our enjoyment of fiction, and that even if we haven't been to a place we can somehow sense whether the writer who describes it has. I remember being in Brazil (or do I?) ten years ago, and the Brazilian literary community being much exercised by John Updike, who'd just published a novel called *Brazil*. ''E was only 'ere a week! One week!' expostulated my genial translator, Hamilton dos Santos. What he would've made of Terry Gilliam's film of the same name I shudder to think, set as it was almost entirely inside the cooling tower of Chiswick Power Station.

No, when a writer's frauds become too flagrant there can only be one solution: send them to Botany Bay. And I'm not talking New South Wales here, but Botany Bay near Enfield. This little village was dubbed by a Victorian wag who found it inconceivably far from London, and the name stuck. Graham Greene would've been perfectly happy in exile there penning a great Australian novel.

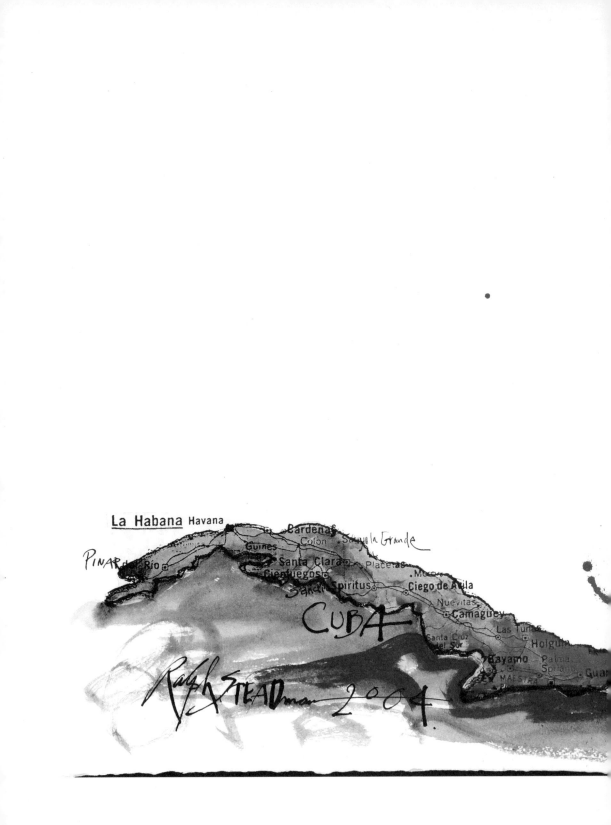

# Line of Control

In February 2002 I was in India, visiting an arms fair to make a film about the death-metal trade for the BBC. It was a sensitive time. In Kashmir a million troops were massed along a euphemism, the so-called 'Line of Control', while the two subcontinental nuclear powers rattled their plutonium sabres with unashamed glee. It was a tense time for me, too. Before leaving London I'd visited the BBC's medical unit, which was housed in a steel-clad, paint-by-numbers block under the lip of the Westway. Here I'd been given a galaxy of shots – for cholera, typhoid, hepatitis and God knows what else – as well a small rucksack full of malaria pills. It hardly seemed necessary for a four-day sojourn in the developing world. (Another great euphemism: if somewhere with a five-thousand-year continuous civilisation is the 'developing' world then what does that make Britain, the 'foetal' world?)

Together with the director, Amir, a charming, faun-like Anglo-Iranian, and David, the cameraman, an avuncular presence, I was holed up in a vast New Delhi hotel. Laid out on two storeys in a series of bewilderingly similar corridors and halls, the hotel reminded me of an Escher print, and as I made the trek to my room I kept expecting to see my doppelgänger disappearing around the next corner.

On the first evening we met up with our local fixer, and the four of us headed out to dinner at a restaurant of great repute. Suddenly we were plunged from the mock-oriental straight into the real thing. It was the first time I'd been in India since the 1980s and while I hadn't forgotten the visceral impact of the place it still came as a shock when we climbed out of the taxi and met a forest of begging arms, many of them deformed. The sheer unadulterated hugger-mugger of old Delhi with its tuk-tuks, naked light bulbs, mud walls and teeming, pan-chewing humanity surged in on me like a wave. Then, sitting in the restaurant, I had a

gastro-epiphany, registering the exact moment when a bacillus crawled off my fork and into my mouth. Sod it, I thought, in for a rupee in for a lakh, and I kept on eating.

The following day as we stalked the arms fair, trying to get oleaginous Department of Trade and Industry wonks and British Aerospace Systems salesmen to talk to us, my innards dissolved into a muddy flux. 'You too?' I squealed at Amir as we dashed between aisles of machine guns and missiles to the khazi. He nodded in pained acknowledgement. But when we both emerged he had in his hand a capsule as big as a smart bomb. 'Take this,' he told me. 'The BBC gave it to me; it's so strong that it'll kill any known stomach bug stone dead in twenty-four hours.'

'Why didn't they give me one?' I wailed petulantly.

'Look,' he thrust it at me, 'I'm giving it to you now – take it!'

The next twenty-four hours saw Amir and me reach a state of considerable nervous hilarity as we attempted to interview reluctant arms traders while breaking off every ten minutes to answer the anguished howl of our diseased natures. We were reduced to spoofing the death-metal dealers – on camera – with a series of skits which we thought wildly funny:

Self: (to Swedish artillery manufacturer standing in front of a model of one of his guns) Is that the actual size of the 200mm Bofors?
Swede: Um . . . no . . . it would not be operational at that size.

Self: (to Finnish camouflage specialist) What's the biggest thing anyone's ever asked you to camouflage?
Finn: Um . . . I don't know . . .
Self: How about a whole country, could you do that?
Finn: Well . . . it would be . . .
Self: Could you camouflage a whole country as another country?

Self: (to South African sniper rifle salesman) Tell me a little about this one.
South African: The Springbok 8809 is a versatile, laser-targeted weapon capable of 99 per cent accuracy at a range of two kilometres.
Self: So in your opinion would this be the right weapon to hit someone in a motorcade?
SA: Errr . . . I guess.
Self: Like a head of state?
SA: You could do that.

Self: For instance . . . Robert Mugabe?

SA: Robert Mugabe?

Self: Yes, he's up that river operating without any control at all and we're going to terminate him . . . with extreme prejudice.

Needless to say, none of this made it on to the box – but at least the Delhi belly was forced back up its line of control. But a week later we were back in England, and I had to raise a delicate matter with Amir.

'Have you, um . . . been burping sort of sulphurously?'

'Yup – you too? It must be because those pills have worn off.'

'Yeah, either that or we've been internally camouflaged by a miniaturised special forces unit.'

'As a volcano?'

'Yeah, obviously, as a volcano.'

'Best call Geoff Hoon* then.'

'Yeah, yeah, better had.'

* Then British Defence Secretary.

# Tea Towel Archipelago

I was standing at the bar of the Taversoe Hotel on the northern isle of Rousay in the Orkneys. My interlocutor had the slushy vowels and beetling brows of a local. 'Where're you going on holiday then, Will?' he asked. 'The Scilly Isles,' I replied. The Orcadian peered for a while into his glass of Dark Island stout, a brew as black as the heart of a berserker, before replying, 'That's not just silly – it's fucking stupid.'

I could see his point. From the vantage of the Orkneys, where the wind only stills for 2 per cent of the average year and the lethal swell of the Pentland Firth crashes against the 600-feet-high cliffs of Hoy, the Scillies not only appear remote but also implausible. In my mind's eye I could visualise a few flower-patterned handkerchiefs of land crumpled in balmy waves; Harold Wilson – the last British Prime Minister who could conceivably be described as 'cute' – sat puffing a pipe in the garden of a bungalow submerged beneath running roses; dwarf cattle wended o'er the lea; a hippy made hay with a pitchfork the size of a table fork. The whole archipelago was so dinky that it could be placed on a tea towel and flogged to a tourist.

Boarding the Scillonian at Penzance I found myself in an island fugue. The ferry looked stubby compared to other, similar vessels, high in the water and a short jog from bow to stern. Across the bay St Michael's Mount rose out of the surf, a tidal nipple of an isle, prinked from the swelling breast of mother England. The Scillonian cast off and within twenty minutes it was rollicking around the long Atlantic swell. I began to feel sick, very sick.

The Scilly Isles are the last vertebra in the long, bumpy spine of Cornwall. These dinky nibblets of land – St Mary's, St Martin's, Tresco, Bryher et al. – are all that are left of a decent-sized island, Ennor, that was gradually submerged between the end of the last Ice Age and 2,000 BC. Ancient field systems can still be traced below the lagoon of St Mary's Bay, and there are sufficient dolmens, tombs and cryptic maze formations to give the islands a satisfyingly mythical cast. John Fowles believes that Shakespeare had them in mind when he was location-spotting for *The Tempest*. Bermuda is the other island that lays claim to the play, and personally I think the two populations should fight it out between them using only whatever magical powers they possess.

I found the Scillies to be quite as twee as I expected – although far more beautiful. They really are stupendously lush in high summer, the teensy fields bursting with a host of flower and plant varieties not ordinarily seen outside the greenhouse. With no motor vehicles at all – except on St Mary's, the biggest island – and everything not simply within walking, but even strolling distance, it was hard not to view the place as not so much a land mass as a scale joke. Pottering out to Porthellick, I was startled by the clatter of the twin-rotor helicopter which is the only other way of getting to the Scillies besides the ferry. I half expected the massive whirligig to let down a hawser, then winch the island to safety.

I've no doubt that when all the tourists are gone the islanders pack the clotted cream fudge away and revert to aggressive type. After all, it was Porthellick where Sir Cloudesley Shovell swam ashore after the wreck of HMS *Association* and two other ships of the line in 1707. The Scilly woman who found him promptly beat him to death and nicked his emerald rings. This disaster cost two thousand lives and demonstrated the absolute necessity for an effective method of calculating longitude. Still, perfectly calibrated chronometers, compasses and GPS didn't stop a Polish freighter, the *Cita*, being wrecked off St Mary's in the 1990s. I bought a little booklet about the wreck in the local bookshop and gathered that it had happened because the ship's master fell asleep at the wheel somewhere in the region of the Strait of Gibraltar. The ship's automatic pilot managed to get it all the way round the Iberian peninsula, across the Bay of Biscay and the Channel, but sadly hadn't factored these flyspecks of land into its computations.

The islanders benefited to the tune of a superfluity of Jack Daniel's, mahogany doors, trainers and car batteries. Of course, in the Orkneys orientation is a tad more robust. When I lived on Rousay there was one celebrated local who'd arrived a few years before from London, having sailed a Thames barge the entire way. Boarded by the coastguard off Peterhead in a Force 10, he was found to be setting his course for the flat-bottomed craft with a map of the Orkneys printed on a tea towel.

THIS is SCILLY!

# Tsunami

The 'Surfers' television commercial for Guinness beer was voted – by members of the public who, bizarrely, care enough about these things – 'The Best Advert of All Time'. But I too found it compelling, and in the wake of the hideously destructive tsunami I find myself pondering again why it is that this filmkin should have such a visceral appeal.

For those of you not familiar with it, *Surfers* is, as its title suggests, a seconds-long drama in which a brawny young man – together with his sinewy pals – catches a massive wave. And I mean massive: if this were a real-life wave it would require a 9.4 Richter Scale earthquake to generate it. The surfer bests the wave, sliding down its great, dark flank in a white spume of spray. Shadowy stallions tossing their manes begin to emerge – in a subliminal kind of way – from the breaking wall of water, and yet our man holds his course and even manages to strike some attitudes. The soundtrack accompanying this feat is a mounting crescendo of bass and drums. Resolution comes: the surfers gain the beach, the stallions subside into the undertow, the tap drips its final dark jewel of Guinness and the glass is set up for our adoration.

I think the reasons this advert is so admired have nothing to do with Guinness itself. 'Surfers' is a timeless evocation of humankind's Promethean urge to master natural forces. The surf, the stallions – they are both wild aspects of a world to be tamed – and when they are we rejoice with a tall glass of dark ale. Sadly, real life isn't always like the movies – or the adverts for that matter. In a piffling, prosaic way I wonder if 'Surfers' will continue to hold on to its No. 1 spot post-tsunami, or if at this very moment the 'creatives' responsible for the Guinness account are pondering how stout adverts will never be the same again; in much the same way that commentators anticipated a re-evaluation of all imaginative values post-9/11.

And what about Hokusai prints? As a child I was fascinated by a portfolio of these belonging to my mother: the empurpled, anfractuous waves; the black, rapier-like boats; the enormous tension implied by so much movement depicted with such a static line. In Japan, where tsunamis are frequent, they have no problem with wavy art – but then this is a culture where the meaningful coexistence of savagery and beauty is, perhaps, better understood. According to the Tao there can be little distinction between the surfers and the wave, when it comes to intentionality.

Personally, great waves have always scared the shit out of me. As a child I imagined death itself in the guise of one, rising up out of the shallow bottom of the North Sea and tilting the Thames Valley region into its own basin. As I grew, so the wavy representations washed over me: Peter Weir's *The Last Wave*, in which and Aboriginal juju summons a tsunami to devastate Sydney; Katharine Bigelow's *Point Break*, in which maverick surfers pull bank jobs in order to finance their quest for the ultimate, gnarly experience; and even John Martin's *The Fall of*

*Babylon*, a nineteenth-century vision of the apocalypse as a watery tumult, spumy masonry and stony whirlpools. The first time I saw this painting (which hangs in Tate Britain) I was transfixed by it, and remained gawping for hours until forcibly removed by the staff.

The word is that avid surfers have been quick to claim that, had they been in the Indian Ocean in the right place, at the right time, they wouldn't have hesitated to try and ride the tsunami. I don't doubt it. Surfing is synonymous with risk and adrenalin junkies are the same as any others: they always require a bigger hit. I remember it used to be the Severn tidal bore that they were always attempting to ride, but presumably this is now viewed as small beer. When I lived in Australia I felt driven to at least try and surf, but my inability to read waves correctly cost me dear and I was unceremoniously dumped. This is when the wave collapses in on itself instead of cleanly breaking, and drives the foolish surfer straight down into the seabed. I was under for long seconds, nearly concussed and was lucky to escape with a wrenched back. In Canberra an osteopath jumped on my crotch and then relieved me of $80.

All of this is by way of saying that nothing can remain off limits. We plant once more on the slopes of Vesuvius; the tourist returns to the sun recliner and the fishermen to the sea. Hokusai sends out for new horsehair brushes and a big pot of blue paint.

# Rotten Smoke

I once visited the Netherlands three times in one year, which, frankly, is pushing it. The third time I went I was met by a Dutchman at the airport. We were queuing to get a car park ticket when I dropped the English Sunday newspaper I'd been reading and its thirty-seven property sections flooded across the floor. One of a pair of burly fellows who were behind us in the queue muttered to his companion 'Zwaar', and they both dissolved into Low Church giggles. As I picked up the newsprint I asked my Dutchman: 'What does that mean?' And he replied, 'Heavy'. That to me encapsulates the Dutch sense of humour: the pratfall is conceived of as ironic. It's a form of Little Country Blues that's oddly – if painfully – endearing.

In the Year of Three Trips, the last time I went by ferry from Margate to Zeebrugge, then drove through Belgium to Rotterdam. My girlfriend at the time discovered when we reached Margate that she'd forgotten her passport. We decided to wing it and she attempted to enter Europe using a British Library card – arguably a more impressive travel document. Belgian immigration wasn't impressed and deported her. The official sneered, 'If only your Mr Major would ratify the EU Treaty these problems would, I think, not be happening!'

I felt so implicated in Britishness that I misguidedly phoned 'our' consul. His answering machine barked, 'Don't bother me with trivial problems like mislaid passports!' I left an 'umble message to the effect that we were having problems entering the country, but don't bother doing anything if it's a hassle – and to our surprise he called back three minutes later. 'What the bloody hell do you mean bothering me with this!' he screamed down the phone. 'I've been up all night scraping four of your fellow countrymen off the central reservation of a Belgian motorway!' I couldn't help but thrill to his flagrant lack of diplomacy.

In truth, this nether-Netherlands visit was a bit of a cliché. I was writing a parody of a James Bond story and decided to set it among the dope-growing

STONED in AMSTERDAM..

Ralph STEADman 2006

174

fraternity. The premise was simple: Bond falls for a lovely Dutch spy but when he arrives in Holland to investigate the skunk business with her they share a joint and it triggers all of his issues. He sees that his activities as a Lothario are simply the flipside of his misogynism. Packed off to boarding school at an early age, he has never really understood women, and, threatened by them, his priapic progress is nothing but his inability to deal with intimacy. Standing in the opulent Rotterdam hotel room, the gorgeous Dutch spy thrown naked across the silk counterpane in front of him, Bond experiences his first flop-on as his head whirls with disturbing images. I called the story 'Rotten Smoke', from the lines in Shakespeare's sonnet 34: 'To let base clouds o'ertake me in my way / Hiding my bravery in their rotten smoke . . .'

In the interests of verisimilitude I'd arranged through a Dutch friend to meet up with some skunky operatives and learn about the intricacies of the business. The wacky tobacconists lived in a vertiginous old terraced house in the district of Amsterdam known – rather suitably – as *De Pijp* (The Pipe). Naturally they turned out to be about as glamorous as a couple of c.1976 polytechnic students reciting Monty Python's parrot sketch. Yes, they'd got on the wrong end of their product. The house had as well: every nook and cranny stank of skunk and there were about fifty kilos stacked up in Geest banana boxes. In order not to arouse the suspicions of any Dutch narcs who happened to be passing downwind, a ventilation system had been rigged up which continually passed the air through a bucket of bleach.

The grower turned out to be a rather straitlaced young woman from Basingstoke, while the 'taster' was an Austrian short-story writer manqué. He wanted to talk Hemingway – most tedious. Before I left he handed me a bud the size of a baby's fist. 'Make sure you've got your head a few centimetres from the pillow before you toke on this,' he warned me. 'It's that strong.' I did as I was told but all that happened was that my girlfriend's face was transmogrified into a hideous vegetative tangle. Rotten smoke indeed.

Ralph doesn't need to indulge in any artificial stimulants at all, as you can see. I wonder sometimes if, like Obelix, Ralph was dropped in a vat of some hallucinogenic potion when he was a child. It would certainly explain the tortured elasticity of his vision. 'Zwaar', as the Dutch would say.

# The Stones of Rome

At Heathrow it transpired that Ivan's passport was five days out of date. The nice man on the British Airways checkout consulted his big book and even made a call, but there was no way round it. The Italians – schizoid participants in the War on Terror – wouldn't let him in. Looked at one way I could appreciate that Ivan constituted a security risk: he's obsessed by guns, knives and all forms of explosion; he has hardly any impulse control yet can also display preternatural cunning; and he has a naïve faith in an omnipotent deity. Still, he is only seven. So Ivan stayed behind in London with his mother, which left four of us to carry on: the big children, little Luther, aged three, and me.

City breaks are quite the thing in our culture, crazed as it is with its own mad sense of alacrity. In this era of Europe's integration its principal cities are being mashed together in the minds of its bourgeois citizens. The Rambla leads to Hradčany Castle; the Herengracht runs through the Tiergarten; and the Spanish Steps ascend the Eiffel Tower. The city break has never appealed to me that much – living in London is quite fracturing enough – but when the opportunity came up to defray travel costs to Rome against a literary reading, we decided to go. After all, what could be more surreal than a speedy sojourn in the cockpit of those ancient modernists the Romans?

Reading Gibbon's *Decline and Fall*, it always occurred to me that the reason Rome took so long in the falling – given that whole provinces regularly went AWOL – was the comparatively slow communications system. Introduce a single phone exchange, with party lines in Scythia, Dacia, Gaul and Egypt, and the Empire would've folded in weeks. You can only fool some of the mob for some of the time. I'd visited the city once before – for six hours to interview the porn-star-turned-politician Cicciolina – yet even this had been long enough to grasp that its sobriquet 'Eternal' was justified. (I mean to say, La Cicciolina herself,

DOWNWARDLY MOBILE

although Czech by birth, would be quite at home in the pages of Petronius.) A whole weekend confirmed my suspicion that Rome remains impervious to the march of time.

There was the metro to begin with. We were staying in Testaccio, the proudly nativist *quartier*, named after the great midden of shattered amphorae, which was the eighth hill of the ancient city (it means, literally, 'mound of sherds'). Our local metro stop was Piramide – and is a dirty great pyramid incorporated into the Antonine wall of the city. It was difficult to believe we were entering a state-of-the-art transport hub under the austere façade of this obelisk, the tomb of an obscure second-century magistrate gripped by the Egyptology craze of his day (thus it's basically an ancient chunk of Tudorbethan). The trains themselves were reassuringly spray-painted with graffiti, but our first stop was Circo Massimo and our second Colosseo. By the time we changed at Termini, all I could think about was that the two arms of the system – Linea A and B – insistently reminded me of the names for the ancient Minoan scripts deciphered by Michael Ventris.

We did the obligatory round: the Colosseum, the Pantheon, St Peter's, the Trevi Fountain, the Spanish Steps, Prada, Bulgari. That night, with the children asleep, I was lying on my bed in the failed post-modern Abitart Hotel (after all, with no modernism, the post- becomes the most proleptic of prefixes), musing on the way the view from the Capitoline Hill drenches the eye with two millennia of civilisation. In London we always think of ourselves as a two-thousand-year-old city, but the truth is that the vast bulk of the burgh is nineteenth-century red brick, bits of the Midlands reshaped and lain in orderly courses. If you want the real McCoy – all flight paths lead to Rome.

The following evening I gave my reading in a teensy theatre in Testaccio. On before me were a collective of hip young writers who called themselves 'Babette's Factory'. Like all Italian intellectuals they wore tweed jackets and brogues, but as a sign of their crazy modernism they also sported odd sprigs of facial hair. They took it in turns to declaim in front of a screen upon which was back-projected pulsating blobs of light. A muted jazz soundtrack accompanied them. I felt as if I were in San Francisco, in the City Lights bookstore, *c.* 1955. I wanted to beat my wine jug on the floor and yell, 'Go man! Go!'

Afterwards the festival organiser explained the recherché character of the event and confirmed my thesis: 'Basically,' he said, 'Italian literature hasn't really had modernism yet. They had a little bit of Futurism and then fascism instead. The whole scene is petrified.' Petrified, yes, but with the kind of petrification Rome offers who needs mere fluidity?

# Foulness

The landlord of the George & Dragon was wary; his voice dropped in tone – almost as if afraid of being overheard: 'Oh no, no – you can't go up there, they wouldn't like it.' He elaborated. 'They'll think you're looking in through their windows, you might not mean to do it – but you will, and then . . . well, then they'll call Security.' I had only suggested that I might leave the pub in Churchend and cycle up to the next village, Courtsend, but clearly this would be a mile too far. Up until that moment I'd known I was in as strange a place as you can reach in an hour by train from London – but suddenly things had turned weird.

The landlord said I was allowed to cycle down to the quay, so I did. It was a half-mile or so, past the church of St Mary the Virgin, past the old primary school which had been converted into a 'heritage centre', past the gates to one of the strange complexes of concrete buildings which studded the green fields of the island. I cycled through a deserted farmyard; in the bare branches of the surrounding trees were huge rooks' nests and the glossy, blue-black birds circled around me as I pedalled, relentlessly kraarking.

At the quay I sat and looked west to where the sun was setting behind a cloud, sending down a perfect fan of rays: violet, grey and pearly pink. At my feet the wide creek purled, the muddy banks were smooth and silvery. Geese clamoured overhead, while in the far distance the dwarfish tower blocks of Southend-on-Sea chewed on the horizon like the snaggle teeth of a senescent world. I felt altogether at peace in this place of war.

Foulness Island – I'd known about it for years. It was a place where sky, sea and mud merged; at once within easy reach and totally inaccessible. Over the years I'd picked up other dribs of information. I knew that the island – the largest off the Essex coast – was wholly owned by the Ministry of Defence and that there were still villages and farms on it, but it wasn't until recently that I learned you could actually visit the place.

All you had to do, it transpired, was phone the landlord of the George and Dragon and ask him to put your name on the gate. Drinking by appointment – surely the ultimate licensing law. I pitched up late afternoon and a bored security guard signed me in. This being 2005 the MoD have passed management of the 10,000 acres of firing ranges and fields over to a private company, Qinetiqa. 'Welcome to Foulness Island' an electronic signboard greeted me as I pedalled off down a military road ruled straight across the flat landscape.

At first sight the island didn't look that peculiar. I mean, not that peculiar if you're familiar with quite how peculiar this part of the British coastline can be: to the north was Dengemarsh – of fever fame – an introverted empty quarter of dykes and isolated farmhouses. To the south, across the Thames estuary in Kent, was the Isle of Grain, where chav meets *Deliverance* in a duel of Burberry banjos.

I passed signs to 'New England' and 'Havengore' – both names of firing ranges. In the distance I could hear the sound of gunfire; in this bucolic context it sounded no more threatening than someone repeatedly slamming a car door. Somewhere to the south, out on the great morass of Maplin Sands, Britain's biggest colony of avocets were wading and dipping. Isolated farmhouses stood kilometres off from the road, gaunt, austere buildings, their windows no more inviting than the cameras oddly angled over steel barriers, and fixed there – I later realised – to record the impact of artillery shells.

I cycled into Churchend. The weatherboard, white-painted houses were all a tad uniform and perhaps their gardens a shade too neat, but it still looked like a real village – not Midwich. It was only chatting to Fred Farenden, the landlord, in the snug of his beautiful 1659 inn that the strangeness of the place started to well over me. Fred is a rubicund and welcoming fellow, but the tale he had to tell was of enterprise constantly thwarted by indifference and bureaucratic meddling. He'd tried bird-watching weekends, B&B packages, and now he was even brewing his own beer – Beaters' Best – but all to no avail. He still had the same sized clientele that he'd had when he first came twenty-four years before: a handful of curious trippers and yachties in the summer, then the long, quiet months of the winter.

Personally I was at a loss to understand it. It might've taken me thirty-five years to get to Foulness – but now I'd arrived I couldn't conceive of any other place I'd rather be.

# Spain – the Final Frontier

It appears that my generation – and the two or three which preceded us – were entirely wrong; far from space being the final frontier, it transpires that Spain is. Far more human effort, ingenuity and sheer dosh is being expended to send men and women to Spain than ever was putting them into space. The computing power tied up in the air traffic control mainframes, automatic pilots, baggage handling systems, on the laps of hundreds of airline passengers en route to Madrid, Barcelona and perhaps even Bilbao – completely dwarfs the dear little IBM machines which were used to crunch the numbers necessary to traject Armstrong, Aldrin and their shipmates. to the moon. I doubt you'd even be able to play Space Invaders with the pile of clunker they had at Cape Kennedy in 1969.

In the 1970s we all fondly imagined that Spain had been conquered. Been there – done that straw hat. Spain was so passé, so colonised, that there was even a Carry On film about hapless Brits pitching up on the Costa Blanca to find their hotel not yet built. Space, on the other hand, was wide open: the moon had been visited, golf had been played there, a dune buggy driven and a rigid Stars and Stripes raised. By the standards of more recent American colonial ventures this may seem pretty convincing – but we knew that there was much more infrastructure to come. First an orbiting space station where the interplanetary craft would be built, then Mars, then Venus.

Suspended animation and nuclear power were the key: knock those super-fit boffins out, tuck them in to chilly sarcophaguses, then power up the plutonium. Bosh-bosh-bosh. Why go to Spain when you could loop your spaceship round Neptune and, using the gargantuan ergs of inertia, whip like stone from a multi-million-mile-long slingshot towards Betelgeuse! Ah, the sights we were going to see, the Asteroid Belt, the Rings of Saturn (these from Ganymede, where we'd have an echoing dinner with an old buffer in a dressing gown), the Horsehead Nebula,

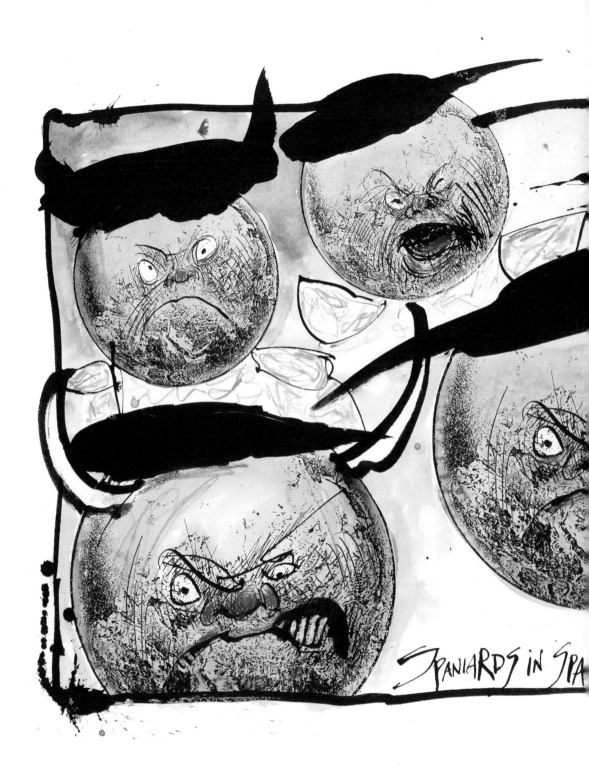

SPANIARDS iN SPA

black holes . . . And because we'd be gone for so many thousands of earth years – while only ageing a few of our own – when we returned we'd find Spain entirely concreted over, and Soylent Green the only tapas available.

So entirely has that *ad astra per aspera* urge been sucked out of us that even to set this stuff down looks pathetic. From the standpoint of an era when Spain is the final frontier, space looks hopelessly archaic – provincial even. Can you sell time shares there? Can you look to it for a renaissance in the cinematic arts or fashion? Has space even got a cuisine to speak of? Fat chance of getting Frank Gehry to build a signature building in . . . don't make me laugh . . . space. Spain, by contrast, has become everything space once promised to be, an almost infinite realm of possibility on to which human aspirations of all kinds can be projected. There is a posh Spain and a poor Spain, a gay Spain and a straight Spain, an urban, bustling Spain and a parched, deserted Spain. Some speculative thinkers have wondered whether or not Spain has any intrinsic character – such is its great diversity.

There is, however, one regard in which Spain can never hope to eclipse space, and that is as a realm of nightmarish terror and extreme privation in which an unprotected traveller can last only seconds before his lungs explode and he drowns in his own blood. True, Spain can be tough. I have spent that night in a cheap bodega in Valladolid, I have witnessed the shaming, alien beauties of Seville – and I well remember the dreadful premonition visited on me in a bank queue in Grenada in 1980. I was standing there with a fistful of traveller's cheques when in came a doddering Brit remittance man. How could I tell this? Simple really: he wore a Burton suit contemporary with George Orwell, was carrying a BOAC flight bag full of empty wine bottles, and began to argue in pidgin Spanish with the cashier about a bank transfer from London. I thought: if I don't get the fuck out of this country immediately I'm going to end up exactly like that, a shameful dipsomaniac paid to stay abroad by his own relatives. I went immediately to the station and hopped trains nonstop back across Europe.

It wasn't until years later that I realised I hadn't escaped my fate at all but rather, like Polybus, I'd run into my homicidal son on the way to Thebes. For I had become the shaky geezer arguing with the cashier – I just hadn't had to move to Spain to do it. Then I understood what futurologists meant when they spoke of 'innerSpain', a realm inside the psyche within which we may travel to meet our destiny, both as a species and as individuals.

# In the Garden

My friends Tony and Elaine have hit upon the ultimate solution to gardening – they've carpeted their backyard. When they moved in a couple of years ago they told me laying this fifteen-foot-square offcut was purely to stifle the great hanks of bindweed which infested the little plot, and soon they'd begin tilling with a vengeance. Recently, however, they've discussed recarpeting the garden on account of the stench of rotten underlay. Well, to carpet your garden once may be a weedkiller, but to carpet it twice looks suspiciously like a lifestyle.

Not that I'm critical you understand – on the contrary; with its twist pile, its set of white plastic chairs, its wonky wooden table and tattered parasol, Tony and Elaine's garden has the virtue of making explicit what is implicit in most suburban gardens. Namely, that these are really outdoor rooms, as far removed from the grandeur of nature as Jack Straw* is from statesmanship. Besides, they're only part of a growing trend: modern gardens are chock-full of furniture, pergolas, loggias, decks, outdoor heaters, lamps, barbecues, Jacuzzis and giant candles. They mostly make little pretence to be anything other than roofless rumpus rooms where the lighting and temperature control are subject to cosmic vagary.

I'm not talking about serious gardens here, the kind tended by people who read books on the subject, but the family garden where dogs, kids and sunburnt drunks graze in uneasy proximity. My own awkward relationship with gardens is rooted in childhood. We lived in a high-privet-density location; the hedges were privet and such was the mania for topiary that it was often difficult to tell whether the woman in the green coat, or the green car gliding past in the road, were real or slightly shaggy simulacra, artfully shaped and then mysteriously animated. My father had little time for gardening, although he quite liked to quote Tennyson. 'Come into

* Then British Foreign Secretary.

CAPABILITY SELF

the garden, Maud,' he would declaim, and my mother would inevitably complete the couplet: 'And mow the fucking lawn.'

Mow the lawn and, of course, clip the hedges. Mother did try with the garden. She got us kids to dig up a bed and grow nasturtiums, tomato plants and runner beans. She had a chequerboard terrace lain with oblong, concrete slabs; then planted geraniums in the oblong beds. Then she held drinks parties at which she wore a muumuu and served Chianti (this was, after all, the 1970s). By contrast I liked nailing odd bits of wood to the oak tree, hurling rowan berries like grapeshot and digging holes. Bigger and bigger holes, until aged thirteen and heavily under the influence of Terry Jacks' seminal death ditty 'Seasons in the Sun', I dug a hole in the garden so deep that I needed a ladder to descend to the bottom and props to prevent subsidence. I only stopped when I hit the water table – try doing that in a contemporary garden!

In retrospect it wasn't so much a grave I was trying to dig as an escape tunnel. I wanted out of suburbia so bad it hurt. I wanted to go somewhere – anywhere – where there weren't so many contentious allotments. I needed money to do this, so I had to go from door to door hawking the only skill I had – gardening. Well, skill is perhaps an overstatement: I could mow lawns and clip hedges, I could weed too, but having been told early on that a weed was only a flower in the wrong place, I subscribed to the view that pretty much everything in the garden should come up forthwith. On the whole the punters were pleased with my services. I suspect they, like me, wanted the geometric lines of their own living rooms ruled on to this obdurate vegetation. However, one man saw fit to express his dissatisfaction (when I'd transformed his head-high rhododendron bush into a squat, black stump) by chasing me down the road wielding the very electric clippers I'd so effectively employed.

None of this is to say that I don't enjoy a garden – I do. I can even be moved to undertake my own improvements. Living in Oxfordshire in the early 1990s, I felt driven to construct a large fence around the orchard which surrounded our house. I bought fence posts, a sledgehammer, tinkling bundles of wire fencing. I dug, hammered and strung for what seemed like – and in fact were – months. I felt like Levin in *Anna Karenina*, reconnecting with my sturdy, peasant roots. The aim of the fence was to stop the children getting on to the farm track – but amazingly they contrived somehow to step through the strands of wire. Fiendish little devils. After this fiasco, Levin spent the better part of the winter in his study, experimenting with his seed drill in ways that its manufacturer had not intended.

# Tea Time in Turkey

It's no messing with Ralph's Turkish black tea. We spoke yesterday on the phone to catch up after his return from holidaying in a Brutalist concrete block near Antalya. The Great Cham was largely confined – he told me – to the hotel compound by armed guards, where he was compelled to amuse himself by shooting people in the bum with an airgun. He did, however, manage to escape to the bazaar where he bought me an impressive meerschaum pipe carved so as to resemble a Turk's head (not a kind of knot, you understand – the real thing).

Meerschaum is as Turkish as Kurdish human rights abuses, and large quantities of this hydrous silicate of magnesium are to be found along its coastline. The locals gather up the clayey mass and transform it into smoking instruments shaped like Kemal Atatürk, Jerry Lee Lewis, Iris Murdoch – indeed, just about any personage they take a fancy to. But I digress. It was the tea that gripped me, and Ralph, ever obliging, shot me a packet up by mail and I'm drinking a glass as I write this.

Turkish black tea got me through the whirling of the dervishes during Ramadan in Konya, central Anatolia; just as gallons of milky tchai sustained me on my treks into the Himalaya, and tiny bowls of fragrant green tea kept me chaste among the sex shows of Patpong. In Morocco it's *thé à la menthe*, in Belfast it's earthy Nam Barrie; indeed, I wonder if there's any region – no matter how hostile – which cannot be braved given the requisite infusion? A cup of tea is both of this world and resolutely out of it; it's a sideways step into a relaxing realm where time stands still for a few minutes.

The growing ubiquity of coffee is a testimony to the gathering pace of globalisation. The best espresso – say a tiny goblet of black go-go mud in Rome's Tazze d'Oro – should be belted down, as its name implies, not mulled over; and while coffee preparation and blends may have their regional distinctions, they are being

speedily and effectively annihilated by the Republic of Caffeine. Not so tea. We acquire a taste for coffee in late adolescence, when we leave home to join the Family of Man, but tea we imbibe with our mother's milk.

Or father's. My own had such a rigid view of his tea ceremonial that he might have been the Confucian sitting under the mulberry tree depicted on the caddy. The pot had to be warmed with boiling water before the leaves were placed in it (leaves – never bags; bags were as alien to him as crack cocaine or pederasty). Milk had to go in the cup before the tea was poured, then three cups were to be drunk – no more, no less. My father swore he could taste the difference if any one of these operations was altered. When I was about seven, he took me to Speakers' Corner to witness British freedom of speech in action. There were the usual bunch of stepladder orators – Maoists, Bible-huggers, rank crazies – and a most interesting Kenyan gentleman, whose subject was the depredations of imperialism.

'I tell you,' the Kenyan proclaimed, 'when I slaved on the tea estates during the Emergency I did my bit to help my brave brothers in the bush fighting Imperialism, yes I did. Do you want to know what I did?' Of course we did – we were transfixed. 'Every single sack of tea that passed through the shed where I worked I pissed in. Yes I did – I pissed in it heartily, satisfied that it would be ending up in your mouths!' 'Ahem,' my father cleared his throat a little uneasily, 'what an angry chap – don't believe a word of it, I'm sure he's fibbing.'

However, I did believe it. Not only that, I grew to consider it one of the shining lights of British democracy, that we could welcome a former subject to our shores and afford him a platform so he could tell us precisely how he'd pissed all over us. What's more, this nameless Kenyan did more for my appreciation of the significance of world trade than a thousand economics tutorials. I can lift a cup of tea to my lips even now and be pungently reminded of where it comes from.

Which takes us back to Turkey – Istanbul, to be precise – where Ralph was pursued by this tea pedlar with a samovar strapped to his back. Either that's what it is, or it's a prototype, steam-powered jet pack. I too have taken to going about the place with tea-making equipment to hand: a camping gas stove, a small kettle, bag, cups and milk. Friends I'm out walking with scoff when I begin to brew up, but once they're sipping they're infused with gratitude. After all, nothing beats a good cup of tea save for a chimpanzee dressed up as a world leader.

# Deliverance –
# Doggy Style

Tully, northern Queensland, Australia. The sugar mill belches smoke as thick and flocculent as candyfloss. Along Highway 1 from Innisfail, the narrow-gauge tracks incise the bluey tarmac and serpentine trains heavy with the sweetness of cut cane trundle through the endless fields. Sugar cane – humanity's biggest crop, weightier than rice and wheat combined. Strange that a world dedicated to producing so much sweetness should nevertheless seem so sour.

And seldom sourer than in Tully, which, to be frank, is a dump. The old 1950s storefronts are warped and mildewed; the tiny grid of commercial premises feels sunk in desuetude. Within a few blocks the Queensland equivalents of pound shops and greasy spoons have given way to overgrown subdivisions and clapboard houses on knock-kneed stilts. Obese, hydrocephalic types crawl along the side-walks, looking as if they're on their way to audition for a remake of *Deliverance*.

The only tourist attractions in Tully are the sugar mill – which does a tour – and the Big Boot. The Big Boot is the same height as the flood waters which covered Tully during the early 1970s, and from its six-metre summit there are command-ing views of . . . the sugar mill. I'm all for the sugar mill tour but the adolescents are revolting – they want to go white-water rafting. You can see their point; beyond Tully the Walter Hill Range of mountains pushes 1,000 metres up into the cloudy skies, rocky summits draped in rainforest, vertiginous gorges, tumultuous cataracts – a vast wilderness of adrenalin.

I don't want to go white-water rafting. I'm not scared – I can't even get close to being scared; it's just that I'd sooner have my penis severed, varnished and put on sale in a provincial gift shop than entrust my frail form to a tiny rubber boat bouncing down the Tully River, which, given that this is the wettest dry season northern Queensland has ever seen, is approaching full spate. Still – it's not about me, is it? So we go white-water rafting.

WHITE WAAARRGH!

We're issued with wet suits and crash helmets and climb into a bus which jolts us through the cane fields and then up a winding road that coils between dripping trees festooned with lianas. The guides are all limber fellows with plenty of piercings and pigtails. They keep up a running commentary the whole way there: if you fall in stay on your back so that if you hit anything it'll be your bottom that takes the impact; choose yourselves a team and get acquainted – your lives will depend upon each other; you must listen to the guide in your boat and do what he says – again, your lives depend upon it. This isn't, it occurs to me, recreation at all; it's survival.

Our team is me, my three adolescents and a mismatched couple from Brisbane: Kurt and Pauline. Kurt is a rugged, good-looking chap. As we carry our raft over the rocks to the river he tells me that the choice was between this and parasailing. Pauline, on the other hand, is so frail, pretty and anaemic that her choices – which manifestly were ignored – must have been between a well-heated art gallery and dabbing eau de cologne on her blue-veined temples.

Our raft guide, a Kiwi called Dan with bleached bits in his hair, urges us to pick a name for our team. 'Somethin' rousing,' he enjoins us, 'so that when we've shot a rapids we can shout it out!' 'Er, how about Deliverance?' I suggest in a desultory fashion, and Kurt, to my considerable relief, sniggers appreciatively. 'Yeah, OK,' says Dan, 'although what I had in mind was, like, "Doggy Style". So that I could shout out, "How d'you like to do it?" – and youse guys would all clash your paddles and shout "Oooh-ooh! Doggy Style!"' As we slip into the brown and white sinewy embrace of the Tully River, I don't exactly feel that Dan and I are on the same wavelength. But, realistically, it's too late for a meeting of minds, because we're in the raft, floating towards the rapids and he's telling me what to do not only for my own survival – but to stop the rest of the team from being dashed to pieces on the rocks.

The strange thing is that it works – the team that is. We paddle when Dan shouts, 'Paddle!' We back-paddle when he shouts that. We shift from side to side in the raft, and as it teeters then plunges over falls we get down in it with our paddles held to attention. At the rapid called 'Wet & Moisty' I fall out of the raft – and the team gets me back in. At 'Double D-Cup' my daughter falls out midway through the cataract and yet is hauled to safety. Whatever our differences concerning nomenclature – it's clear that Dan has the measure of the Tully Gorge.

# Fantastic Mr Fox

Oliver Rackham, the magisterial historian of the English countryside, has several bees in his bonnet. One of them concerns the word 'forest'. If you believe Rackham there's no necessary connection between 'trees' and 'forests'. Forests are areas set aside for the hunting of wild game – deer, boar and suchlike – while wooded areas of country are, doh!, woods. Forests are characterised by their ancient laws and royal-appointed officers, while woods feature toadstools, crapping bears, fairy rings and farouche child abusers.

I love Rackham's writing on the countryside. To read his accounts of woodland management, the structure of field systems and even soil drainage is to have the godlike sensation that when it's all tarmaced over and there's a Tesco Metro where every copse used to be, one could simply reconstruct the whole palimpsest of our biota, using Rackham as a set of instructions. My friend Con has slightly disabused me concerning the omniscience of Rackham. He too is a disciple and once made a pilgrimage to the great seer of the bucolic at Corpus Christi, his Cambridge college. It transpired that Rackham obviously took his agenda from what he could see from the window of his rooms; and that his masterwork, *The History of the Countryside*, should really be called *The History of the Bit of Countryside I Can See from my Window*.

If I animadvert on Rackham it's because of what happened to Mr & Mrs Ralph this week. They awoke during the night to the sound of a loud crash echoing through the vastness of Steadman Towers. On arising they found a trail of bite marks and paw prints leading through the elegant chambers and along the marble colonnades. A large, silk-covered ottoman had been reduced to a tatterdemalion; a turd had been deposited in the toilet. Eventually they cornered the interloper in the kitchen. How a fox cub had had the wit to become housetrained after only that very night entering a house for the first time is a source of wonder to us all.

DOMESTIC
FOX HUNTING

TO the LOOSE MANOR
BORN.

Now, Rackham's take on foxes is sanguine to say the least, given that he views the two cataclysmic events in the English countryside to have happened during the Iron Age, and then in the late nineteenth century. The first was the clearing of the primary woodland, and the second was the turning over of whatever little spinneys remained to the intensive rearing of game birds. Set beside these awesome reductions in biodiversity, the artificial preservation of the fox in order that it may be hunted stands as an amusing little appendix. And preserved it has been. Rackham's hunch is that it would have been extinct in the early-modern period were it not such good fun cornering it on horseback, then watching it being torn to shreds by doggies.

The irony that the fox was preserved for so long that it managed to adapt to the growing urbanisation of England cannot be stressed enough. Over the last few years, during which this environmental appendix became so inflamed that it poisoned the body politic, it was hilarious to hear the fox-hunting lobby bleat on about how they had to hunt foxes in order to a) keep their numbers down, b) keep countryside folks' numbers up. In essence this was the same as a talking hamster telling you that it was essential he kept running round and round in order to preserve his wheel.

Looked at from the point of view of the parasitic fox, the redcoats were a good survival strategy. However, now that you can't walk down a London street without seeing an insouciant fox strolling towards you it's clear that it must be foxes themselves that were behind the whole mad convulsion. While hunting was essential for their survival they happily ripped chickens to pieces and ran amok in the farmyard. But a few years ago a top-flight delegation approached the late Roald Dahl and got him to write *Fantastic Mr Fox* as the first in a string of clever propaganda tricks aimed at ensuring their long-term niche in the human-dominated ecosystem.

Most of the time I feel fairly well disposed to foxes. We often get up in the morning to see two or three of them sunning themselves on the tops of the garden sheds in back of our house. Granted their shit smells dreadful, they rip bin bags open and their sexual behaviour – even by south London standards – is both violent and rambunctious. Still, I saw no need to have them culled for this until the fox got into Ralph's house. After all, to follow Rackham on this, while there may be no necessary connection between forests and trees, the prospect of one's kitchen becoming a game preserve is not a comfortable one. Mark my words, it'll begin with the odd fox breaking in, but before you know it you'll be transported to Australia for laying a hand on one of the Queen's dinosaur-shaped turkey nuggets.

# Feng Shui in Singapore

We stood next to a London cab on the forecourt of the Elizabeth Apartments in the fast-falling dusk of South-East Asia. It was the latest model, a bulbous TX2. Roland Soh, the cabbie, was regarding his vehicle with a certain weary affection. 'This,' he told me, 'is one of the most expensive cabs in the world.' He ran me through the bill for it: $30k for the car certificate, 120 per cent import tax. It all adds up to a cool $120k Singaporean. 'I'm going to sell it next year,' he conceded, 'and get a people carrier.'

We fell in with Mr Soh at Changi Airport, and his London cab, complete with British Lung Foundation sticker on its glass hatch, helped to make landfall that much more uncanny. Singapore struck me immediately as Basingstoke force-fed with pituitary gland. The island is low-lying, greenish and tricked out with corporate bypass architecture: skyscrapers like hypertrophied conservatories hollowed out by truly hideous atriums.

At the Elizabeth Apartments, where we put up, we looked up from the lobby into a void cluttered with thirty-odd concrete balconies; the sky was a mirror, the vending machine offered soft drinks flavoured with chrysanthemums. The apartment itself was all tiled surfaces and heavyset armoires, the TV served up a state-sanctioned diet of Murdochian pap: mobile phone commercials masquerading as news bulletins.

Still, we weren't really in Singapore at all, only stopping over for twenty-four hours. Enough time to crank the kids' body clocks halfway round, so that when they reached the fatal shore they weren't bouncing off the walls with jet lag. Singapore understands its own status as a 300-square-mile holding bay for people. The majority Chinese population throng the streets with their notorious orderliness, while in the lee of the skyscrapers Malays in pyjamas sweep up very little.

Mr Soh explained to me the intricacies of the car certificate. Apparently the government controls exactly how many cars there are at any given time on the island. In order for a new car to be born an old one must die. It strikes me that this is a policy inflected by Confucianism: the orbital road of life whispering on through the eras, symbol and reality interfused. I said as much and Mr Soh smiled in a satisfied way. 'There's more to Singapore,' he told me, 'than meets the eye.'

What does meet the eye is the Merlion: half-lion, half-fish. A chimerical symbol for a chimerical state. The Merlion is everywhere. There are Merlion cruets and mobile phone covers, newel posts and carpet figures. Down at Merlion Park, where the Singapore River meets the sea, a giant Merlion squirted a jet of water into the gloopy atmosphere, while out in the grey bay the ocean-going equivalents of Singapore's skyscrapers oozed along the horizon.

Hungry for the anchor of the past in this rudderless vessel of modernity we headed for Chinatown. Along Smith Street there were reassuring carved house fronts, the city hunching down to a human scale. Atop the Sri Mariamman temple a mosh pit of Hindu deities rose into the drizzle in a tangle of garish concrete limbs. Further down the street, gongs resounded outside the Buddhist temple, where great stooks of fake currency were being consumed by fire. It was easy to understand how the rogue bond trader Nick Leeson – who was based in Singapore – got the idea that money was worthless paper, mere vouchers to be shovelled into the incandescent belly of capitalism.

We ate at the Maxwell Road Food Centre, where all the old Chinese street vendors have been corralled under a cast-iron roof. Down aisles of tripe and along transepts of glazed chicken we strolled: little dumplings of humanity peristalsised by the stomachs of pigs. Full up, we were evacuated and headed for the Lucky Centre so the kids could buy many many cheap wristwatches.

I retailed all of this to Mr Soh as we stood waiting for the rest of the family to join us in the cab and head back to Changi. He was keen to explain the commercial slabs along Orchard Road to me in terms that undercut psychogeography with more ancient and arcane concepts. 'You see the Hyatt Hotel,' he pointed at a liverish porphyry dolmen, 'they built it without consulting the geomancer. The reception desk was at the wrong angle, the entrance was set too far back from the road. It cost them millions in lost revenue before they gave in and had the entire building remodelled. I could give you tens of other examples . . .' He trailed off. It wasn't clear whether Mr Soh was expressing credulousness or its opposite. Whether he thought feng shui was a function of people's perception or an ulterior reality.

As one we reached out to touch the black hide of the cab, so that it could reassure us both with its $120,000 bulk.

The SINGAPORE BELCH

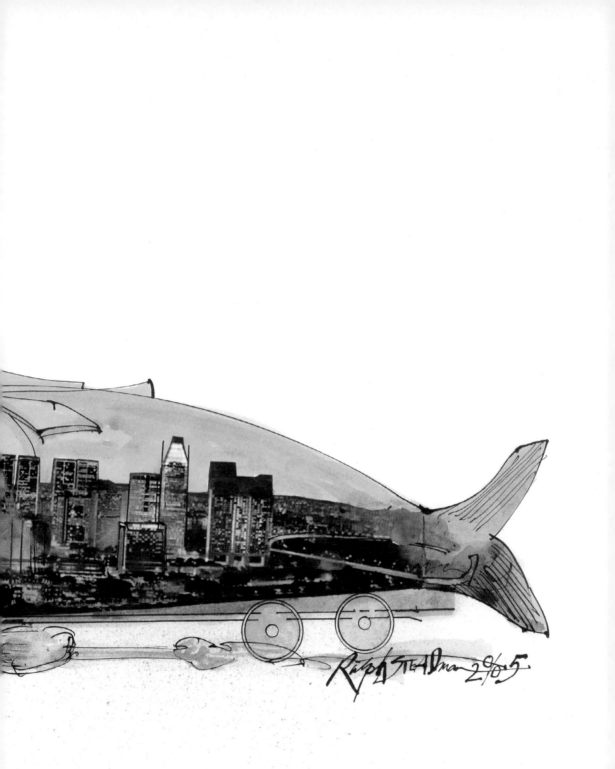

# The Fugitive

Where is Osama bin Laden? I only ask because he's been on the run for years now, and despite the best efforts of the World's Top Power – its heat sensors and attack dogs, its agents and bounty hunters – they seem no nearer to capturing him than they were five or even ten years ago. After 9/11 bin Laden footage was a staple diet for building up our crusading zeal. There he was: the beardie bogeyman, moving with leisurely awkwardness between the rocky defiles of an Afghan moonscape. A stick insect of a man with a Kalashnikov in lieu of a cane, his aquiline – yet bilious – face lean beneath his turban. They seek him here! we cried. They seek him there! They seek him bloody well everywhere! Is he in heaven? Is he in hell? That damned elusive orchestrator of worldwide terror!

The consensus among informed commentators is that bin Laden and Al-Qaeda never really functioned in quite the manner that we'd like. Despite his appearance – straight out of central casting – this softly-spoken fanatic was and is no Dr No, his sensitive fingers poised to activate thousands of loyal henchmen, but instead a kind of venture capitalist of terrorism. If you want to spread anthrax on the metro or port an incendiary backpack, you can apply to the bin Laden organisation for funding and technical know-how. Befitting his background as the scion of a Saudi Arabian construction dynasty, bin Laden is a money rather than an ideas man.

Still, he and his associates do have one implacable idea: that by wreaking death and destruction on the infidel they will awaken the torpid Muslim masses and force them to overturn their corrupt rulers and impose the rule of God. Getting captured would put a severe crimp on this plan, for, so long as bin Laden is at liberty, no matter how circumscribed his personal influence, he acts as a potent figurehead for every ragged man who raises a rocket-propelled grenade launcher to his shoulder and lets fly. His face is on a million T-shirts, his name is constantly on the lips of Iraqi insurgents and Hamas fighters. When Al Jazeera receives a scratchy

videotape or a creaking recording, his omniscience is only confirmed. Nothing is more fitting than that he should be thus: exiguous, wavering, a smoky djinni billowing above the apocalyptic battlefield.

We want him up there in the debatable lands of north-western Pakistan, the savage landscape that swallowed the Great Gamers and spat out the bones. We picture him guarded by fearsome Pathan tribesmen armed with fifteen-foot-long rifles. Although the chances are he's probably in Reigate. In Reigate and spending his days shuttling across to Crawley General Hospital for a little gentle kidney dialysis. In Reigate, and far from bothering with a shave and a haircut – let alone radical cosmetic surgery – I bet he still looks exactly the same. 'Who's that old geezer then?' ask those who see him sitting on a park bench, or abrading a scratch card. 'He don't 'alf look like that bin-whatsit bloke.' To which his unwitting protectors reply: 'Oh him? He's harmless enough – he drinks down the Chequers and plays bowls in the afternoon.' Hardly what you'd expect – his entire disappearing act resting on phenomenal chutzpah.

We want fugitives though. We like the idea that Lord Lucan, Butch Cassidy and Martin Bormann are playing gin rummy at a beachfront bar in Mombasa. We urge the bad guys on across the Rio Grande; we supply plane tickets to sarf London faces so they can take off for the Costa del Crime. So long as there are fugitives in the world there remains a certain mystery at its margins; all has not been discovered, snooped into, X-rayed by the CIA. The capture of the fugitive is always intolerably prosaic – in an instant he is transformed from a figure of dreadful potency into an unshaven old man with plaster dust in his unkempt hair. This phenomenon is perfectly illustrated by Saddam Hussein, and ever since his capture the media have been willing him to assume his former guise: the coal-black moustache of tyranny.

Thus flight is only a good career move if you're prepared to stay on the run indefinitely. Don't end up like Kim Philby, whingeing and drunk in Moscow; or Ronnie Biggs, bartering your freedom for the National Health; or Adolf Eichmann, displayed in a plastic box in Tel Aviv, and such a prosaic figure that Hannah Arendt coined the expression 'the banality of evil' purely in order to describe his showroom-dummy features. Better not to go on the run at all; be like Slobby Milošević, throw your arms up, make them build you a special courtroom in the Lowlands, then spend the next few years on your demented high horse, forcing them to spend billions simply in order to give you a slap.

# Black Cloud

We're always keen to welcome new talent in this column, so it's with great enthusiasm that we introduce to you a great big black cloud of hydrocarbons floating over southern England. Black Cloud – as we'll call it for convenience – first appeared on the morning of Sunday 11 December 2005. My friend Louisa was staying about two miles from Hemel Hempstead when at 6.00 a.m. she was awoken by an earth-shattering explosion: 'The whole house shook on its foundations, some of the windows broke. When we got up and looked to the west there were giant flames lighting up the pre-dawn sky. Naturally our first assumption was that this was a terrorist attack, but when we turned on the TV we discovered that this oil depot had caught fire.'

The Buncefield Oil Depot to be precise. Crazy name – crazy great inland lagoon of highly inflammable petrol and aviation fuel, hundreds of thousands of litres of the gunk. I find the name itself highly suggestive, 'bunce' being City traders' slang for the money they cream off the top of a deal. So a field of bunce suggests a veritable patina of profit dirtying every little living thing. Still, I doubt it's an image that will appeal to the residents of Leverstock Green, who had to be evacuated from their homes as the huge death's head of smoke wobbled up into the sky.

Over the next couple of days while the fire burnt itself out we were treated to a magnificent photo shoot of Black Cloud as it struck various attitudes above the land: Black Cloud boiling and bloody in the immediate vicinity of the burning tanks; Black Cloud lowering and minatory over the bog-standard 1960s semis surrounding the depot; Black Cloud seen from a helicopter at 5,000 feet, a thick discharge of poison rendering the very curvature of the earth itself unstable and problematic. Eventually we were shown a satellite image of Black Cloud hanging over the entire southern half of Britain, a filthy aorta beating in the heart of our green and unpleasant land.

In a year which has been marked by some really exciting disasters, both man-made and natural (although this is, in my view, a specious distinction), it's a great thrill to welcome the greatest explosion in peacetime Europe. It took 150 fire-fighters using 32,000 litres of water every minute to put out the blaze, while they blanketed the storage tanks with a winter wonderland of chemical foam. Up in Black Cloud itself were the equivalent of 25 per cent of a single day's hydrocarbon emissions in the UK.

Put like that it doesn't sound so impressive after all. I mean to say, the spectacle of health official after environmental wonk popping up on our television screens to warn us of the coming sooty Armageddon acquired a certain risible character when the camera cut away to reveal the Hemel Hempsteaders still tooting about in their hydrocarbon-emitting bumper cars immediately beneath the Black Cloud itself.

On the Friday after the explosion at the depot I couldn't resist going to have a look at Black Cloud's theatre of operations. I told my brother I was taking him on a 'mystery walk' in the London environs, and conducted him on to the train at Euston while he averted his eyes from the signboards and hummed during announcements. Detraining at Apsley I told him our destination and we walked on companionably, siblings united in absurdity. It was a perfect sunny winter's day, and not until we were within a stone's chuck of the BP Building which marked the southern edge of the 'control zone' could we smell the rankest of the rank, but the patina of profit was nowhere to be seen.

The cops at the first barricade waved us nonchalantly on after I'd engaged them in a lengthy boring about maps and logistics. At the next roundabout the roadway was heaped with the linguini of flattened hosepipe. There were emergency services vehicles a-flashing, and a cop car started tootling towards us. 'We'll walk towards them,' I told my brother, 'that way they won't get narked.' I flipped my NUJ card and said to the senior officer, 'Press, we just wanted to have a look at the site.'

'You shouldn't be here at all,' he replied.

'Well, we'll just head back the way we came,' I said breezily.

'No, you'll have to be escorted from the area. I've had experience of the press,' this middle-aged Hertfordshire policeman with grey hair and a fluorescent jacket said as if he were a shape-shifting Ingrid Bergman, 'and I've learnt never to trust a single thing you gentlemen say.'

'We aren't those kind of press,' I wheedled.

'No,' my brother put in helpfully, 'I work for *Country Life*.'

We left under a black cloud of disapproval, smothered with the foam of shame, and pursued by distinctly porcine bears.

# The Vatican at Sea

Standing in the Piazza Risorgimento, sorting in a desultory fashion through a box of miniature plaster legionaries priced at 5 euros a pop, I feel none of the excitement I thought I would. I am about to enter the smallest country in the world – yet there is no frisson, no palpitation, no sweat. At 0.17 square miles Vatican City is way out in front when it comes to dinky sovereign states – it makes Liechtenstein look like Canada, Monaco like Russia, Luxembourg another virgin planet. As a connoisseur of all things ickle I feel I have been striving towards this moment all my life, yet now I face the walls of the citadel my spirits are decidedly low.

It could be the queues: the phalanxes of rain-smocked tourists, the crocodiles of hirsute nuns, the camper-van-loads of Scandinavians. It could be the prices: I just fed the children pizza and now my bankroll has anorexia. But on balance I think it's because Vatican City, despite its flag, national anthem, post office, miniature rail system and bijou army of Swiss Guards, has none of the attributes you really expect from a country. To be blunt – it has no hinterland save for a park, and no border controls save for a ticket vendor. Added to this, its principal buildings are way too large.

St Peter's is a power-trip basilica, crazed by its own sense of importance. No self-respecting country dedicates this much masonry to glorifying an immaterial deity. It's as if you pitched up on Easter Island and found a monolithic head four miles high. Besides, Vatican City is but a rump of territoriality, the merest crumb left behind on the Roman table when the rest of the Papal States were snaffled up. Surrounded by a Pacific of masonry, its egregious treasure hoard of books, paintings and jewelled chasubles is in danger of being inundated by a rising tide of atheistic rationalism.

No, when I think of a small country I think of Andorra. Not, you appreciate, that I've ever actually been there, but people do – Barnaby up at the bike shop went there last year for a snowboarding holiday. He said it was fine, relatively cheap, and he felt not the slightest little bit of claustrophobia. My late father always used to tell me that you could roll a marble from one end of Andorra to the other – a feat he claimed to have performed – but I have my doubts about this, as he also believed himself to be descended from the yeti, and to have visited El Dorado (a mythical city he somewhat improbably located on Salisbury Plain).

Or, alternatively, Sealand. Sealand is truly small – it makes Vatican City seem like an illimitable tract of tundra. True, it isn't exactly terra firma, being rather a bizarre, seven-storey naval fort (Roughs Tower) left behind seven miles off Harwich in Essex after the Second World War. Declared a sovereign state by 'Prince' Roy Bates in 1967, Sealand has had a chequered history, including an invasion staged in 1978 by a turncoat German businessman with an army of Dutch mercenaries.

However, Sealand does boast its own currency, postage stamps, flag &c. It has also had de facto recognition of its sovereignty by the British courts (specifically Chelmsford), and so far the Inland Revenue have not sought to levy National Insurance from its citizens – at least when they're in residence of the tower. Bates, a former Second World War airman, founded Sealand on sound libertarian principles, believing that any people should have the right to self-determination on any piece of land not previously claimed. This sits a little oddly beside his royal title, rather as if the Pope claimed that Vatican City only existed so that the young people could copulate freely under the influence of Ecstasy. Stranger still is the assumption of the title Prince Regent by his son Michael, for it was Michael who was kidnapped by the invading cheese heads of '78.

Personally, if I'd spent my childhood being traumatised on a hunk of metal in the North Sea the last thing I'd want to do is become its Prince Regent, but then I suppose I'm not exactly the stuff secessionists are made of. If you walk along the coast of Kent between Whitstable and Herne Bay, or Essex between Clacton and Harwich, you can see these enigmatic Maunsell sea forts studding the beaten pewter of the horizon. They look like Wells's invading Martians, stunned into decades of inanition by the prospect of making a landfall at Margate or Walton-on-the-Naze.

In the 1960s quite a few of the towers were occupied by pirate radio stations but those heady, pop-picking days are over. Sealand survives – wouldn't you guess it – as an offshore e-commerce centre, the Dutch Antilles of the virtual world, but surely there's a case for some of the other towers becoming sovereign states? If the Vatican were to move to one of the sea forts it could only be interpreted as the Church Triumphant – and a massive publicity coup to boot.

# Canalised

Sunday lunch, organic carrion, five others present, as far as I know all of them have good hearing. I say: 'I'm going to cycle from Liverpool, along the ship canal to Manchester tomorrow.' No one acknowledges this, so I say it again: 'I'm going to . . . &c.' It is as if they can't hear me at all, the conversation has passed on – to types of corkscrew, child development, Marx's facial hair (Groucho, not Karl) – leaving me bobbing in its wake. I'm not so foolish as to be unable to comprehend why this should be: my remark is the analogue of the journey it describes. These metropolitan media types might go to Liverpool for an art biennale, or to Manchester for a party conference, but the idea that these two, proximate cities can be journeyed between, purely for the sake of it, is way off the edge of their flat and papery world.

Then there are those other, fatal words: 'cycling' and 'ship' and 'canal'; all guaranteed to make even active minds shut right down. Had I casually let fall that I was going on a rainforest safari with the Ituri pygmies of the Congo, or even, sotto voce, that I was considering two weeks of colonic irrigation in Chiang Mai, they would all have been agog.

So, the following morning, I found myself standing on Runcorn Station having detrained, and the 7.13 to Lime Street was pulling away, and many many thousands of obsolete stair rods had been pressed back into service so that they could rain down on me. Yet, no matter how inauspicious a start, I still felt liberated. Once more I'd pulled it off, and loosed the so-called 'lines of desire' with which urban planners lash us to workplace, retail outlet and real estate.

I assembled the foldaway bike and pedalled away into the maelstrom that howled about the steel girders of the bridge across the swirling, turbid Mersey. I'd abandoned the idea of the full push from the 'pool. I had limited time, and I'm not an amphibian. Nevertheless, I soon felt like one, pumping up the towpath of the St

Helens Canal, my waterproofs as slick as sealskin. The aim of following the ship canal all the way had also been dropped, when the map confirmed what common sense – never my strongest suit – should have told me; namely, that ships don't get towed along paths. Instead, I would follow the Trans Pennine Trail, replete with graffiti-obscured info-boards and shuttered ranger stations.

On I slithered, through a watery world carved by the tail of the Mersey as it lashed in its flood plain. Past the fat-bellied deities of the Runcorn Power Station cooling towers, where I could hear metal being tortured behind closed doors, while steam clouds of preternatural brightness plumped above the reed beds. I may wax lyrical – but then why shouldn't I? When I joined the ship canal itself, at Warrington, I felt my wheel fitting into a groove scoured out over centuries by the most historically significant motive forces Eurasia has ever known.

The ship canal: a pre-rail, eotechnic form of transport, force-fed by coal and steel. Manchester: the manufactory of the world for a hundred years. Liverpool: its port – and the line of the canal – extended in space across the Atlantic to America, like a water spout from a chthonic past shooting into the post-industrial future. And it was, of course, deserted, except for a man walking a Scotty dog under a golfing brolly, his feet crackling on empty White Lightning bottles, while a hubcap gleamed on the eroding bank.

At a massive set of locks, lowered over by a red-brick building bearing the optimistic legend 'New World Gas Cookers', I left the ship canal and followed the route of a dismantled railway across country to Altrincham. The rain cleared and from the embankment I could see jets hurled up by Manchester Airport to spear the cloud cover. I joined the Cheshire Ring Canal for a few miles, before, at Sale, sodden and chapped, deciding to chuck the proverbial towel in. I folded up the bike and boarded a tramcar, which ran up on an elevated section through the outskirts of the conurbation, before, at Old Trafford, suddenly dipping down to the ground and merging with the road traffic.

It was a fitting end to such a journey: the seeming-train transforming into a bus. I had traversed mighty canals that were now weedy backwaters, and the muddy sloughs of defunct iron roads. This part of the world was not a landscape at all, but a palimpsest, worked over again and again by the busy hands of humankind. At dinner that night, in a Thai restaurant, I announced to my five Mancunian companions – none of whom, so far as I know, were hard of hearing – 'I cycled from Runcorn to Sale today.' And this remark went blissfully unacknowledged.

# Middle Earth

Forgive me if I've written this before, but as a man – or a woman, or an hermaphrodite for that matter – grows older, his/her ability to recall things, thankfully, gets hazy. Besides, this was one of the formative experiences of my life, so why not come at it from another angle?

When I worked as a corporate publisher in the 1980s I went to pitch my services to Weetabix, who had their factory in Kettering in the East Midlands. It was the usual tedious drive up into the heart of England, my suit jacket dangling from a hook behind my ear, my face frozen in that dreadful rictus which is engendered by loud in-car entertainment, nicotine, Nescafé and gnawing frustration. When I got to the outskirts of the town I pulled up, and, stepping out of my regulation Ford Sierra, I was assailed by a great wave of wheatiness that engulfed me, stoppering up my mouth and nostrils with the essence of an thousand thousand breakfasts.

Blimey! I thought (these were innocent days, the whole culture existed before the watershed), what can it be like to grow up in this cerealville? As a child, you must believe that this intense, foody atmosphere is natural, then, when at last you reach your maturity, and travel to some other burgh – say Redditch – be altogether perplexed by its absence.

Ever since I've thought of the Midlands as a region dominated by these monoproduct towns: Birmingham for cars, Nottingham for shoes, Bourneville for chocolate, Stafford for pottery. The waist of Olde Englande is cinched by a belt studded with these buckles, and to travel around it is to find yourself in the tarmac aisles of some grossly elongated cash-and-carry. Not that you'll be carrying many cars away from Birmingham nowadays; indeed, so far has the second city shed its status as the Detroit of England that the centre is now almost entirely pedestrianised. Pedestrianised and elevated: the other evening (the first balmy one of summer), I walked all the way from the trendy restaurant area around the canal at Brindley

The PSYCHO-RAMBLER

I BUY TWO AND GET ONE FREE

THUS— FOR THE POOR

REFUTE IT NOT

Ralph STEADman 2006

Place, to my hotel by St Philip's Cathedral, without even setting foot at ground level. Doubtless out at Longbridge the rust never sleeps, while tumbleweeds blow across Spaghetti Junction.

The following morning I left for Lichfield, and sat in the jolting, sunlit carriage assailed by an inane in-train television channel. Who would've thought that the future would be so technologically scrambled? Yes, we anticipated such things in the 1970s, but we thought they'd come together with jet packs, meals-in-a-pill and eternal life. Instead we get stainless-steel automated toilets, embedded in the same old shitty railway platforms.

Such meditations were fit meat for Lichfield, where the pollution-corroded fangs of the perfect bijou Gothic cathedral gnawed at the sky and gnashed on the winding, Tudor-fronted streets. Lichfield being a carpet town, there was its most famous son, Samuel Johnson, looking gloomy, dropsical and depressed, while apparently sitting atop a pile of cheap rugs. On the plinth of the statue which was surrounded on all sides by the carpet market was this epigram of the Great Cham: 'Every man has a lurking wish to appear considerable in his own land.'

'What a deep pile of . . .' I muttered to myself, as I wandered off to find some cheese in a nice olde cheese shop. But there was none to be had anywhere. I consulted an ancient crone of the diocese, who informed me: 'You'll have to go to Iceland.' And that, in a non-recyclable plastic shell, is the very rub of modern Middle England: you always have to go to Iceland.

At the cathedral a genial beadle told me: 'We've a lot of children in today, but I'm sure they won't bother you and nor,' his eyes hardened into paedophilia-seeking devices, 'will you bother them.' Frankly, I would've been hard put to bother them, because there were hundreds of the little blighters. Whole choirs of little seats had been lain out in the nave, the transept, the chapels, and upon them lessons were taking place. What a joy it was to see this magnificent building fully tenanted, instead of vacuous with the absence of God.

I plodded on out of Lichfield as the day heated up. On and on along the canal heading north. On and on past fields of alien, oily rape. On and on, with only my overheated brain for company. Towards late afternoon I crossed over Watling Street and reached the outskirts of Burton-on-Trent, only to be assailed by a great wave of maltiness, a farinaceous swell that engulfed me, stoppering up my mouth and nostrils with the essence of an thousand thousand pints of lager. The great steel vats of the Coors brewery scintillated in the sunshine. 'What must it be like,' I mused, 'to grow up in this beerville, waiting your entire childhood for chucking-out time?'

# Kate Moss or Moss?

Shown here are a group of peasant women Ralph caught on camera during his recent sojourn in the rural fastness of Puglia. According to a local ethnographer (who Ralph managed to corner in a bar, then strong-arm until he divulged), the ancient crones are worshipping a totemic carving of Rianare, the God of Cheap Plane Flights. Their belief is that if a suitable offering is presented to Rianare (a garland festooned with polished olive stones is usually enough), he will bless the donor with a £27.49 return flight to Stansted; or Luton, or Gatwick – and possibly even the East Midlands Airport. Anywhere, in fact, so long as it isn't Heathrow, the passenger wasn't born in a leap year, and their hold baggage doesn't contain more socks than pants. (Pants surcharge is £4,578.23 per pair.)

I myself am a recent convert to the cult of Rianare, having flown to Cork at the weekend on a low-cost airline. In Ireland the God is known as 'Ryanair' (Rían-àr in the original Gaelic), and his devotees, despite the anathema pronounced on them by the Cardinal Primate of All Ireland, are quite as numerous and fanatical as those in southern Italy. Personally, I didn't know what to expect when I started on this new, spiritual path. I had been warned that in return for a seat Ryanair demanded exorbitant mortification on the part of his suppliants. There would be a twenty-mile walk from the departure lounge to the gate. Indeed, very likely there would be no gate at all, simply a gash in the aluminium skin of the terminal building, through which passengers would be bodily hurled on to the concrete apron.

Once on the plane – already battered and bruised – I would find no seats, as such, only straps from which to hang. When turbulence came, us dangling punters would collide with each other like ball-bearings in a Newton's cradle, setting in motion the most inappropriate collisions, and even spontaneous acts of congress. No wonder, I thought, the Cardinal Primate takes such a dim view. Moreover, there would be no strap allocation, for on cheap flights it's every man, woman and

223

even child for themselves. In the event things weren't that bad at all. There were seats, and, as none of these were secured, instead of finding myself sandwiched beside one of my own, needy offspring I instead plumped down and discovered that my thigh was melded against that of Kate Moss, the internationally renowned model and demi-mondaine.

Surprised? I didn't even know she was Irish. It transpired that Moisty – as she is familiarly dubbed – flies back and forth to West Cork with disarming frequency. As she vouchsafed to me, the flights are now so cheap that it's more cost effective for her to hire a babysitter in Bantry and have them flown over for the evening, than to engage one on Primrose Hill. I spoke to a couple of other parents of young children on the flight, and they said the same thing: Ryanair brought families closer together; now Nan could sit, chewing a quid of tobacco, and singing 'The Croppy Boy' in the corner of their Danish Modern kitchen in Clifton, for the price of a loaf of soda bread. Mind you, that isn't for the price of a loaf of soda bread actually on a Ryanair plane; that costs £27,609.43 (€40,653.29).

Who are we environmentalist Cassandras to deny these simple folk their consanguinity admixed with aviation fuel? What perverse ideology would dare to tear grandchild from grandmother, stag night from Cork bar? So what if the improved familial relations of today are ruining it all for succeeding generations? At least those future generations will have had well-adjusted parents. And anyway, the airspace of today is not the airspace of yesteryear. That was a moneyed preserve, accessible only to the super-rich, who in a very important sense owned it. Now the sky belongs to all, and is like unto an illimitable, blue moorland, across which the masses have the inalienable right to roam.

Frankly, this is all just as well, because once you actually arrive in Ireland you will find yourself subject to a most astonishing reversal: you may have been able to fly hundreds of miles with utter abandon, but at ground level the Emerald Isle sets up fierce resistance to the idea of anyone daring to stray off the beaten track. Since 1995 something called the 'Owners Liability Act' has been in force. This makes property owners legally obliged to compensate walkers for any accidents that happen to them on their land – even if these occur on public rights of way. Needless to say, this has made Irish landowners – never that keen on unconstrained roaming in the gloaming – positively Stalinesque, exiling ramblers from their land with brutal alacrity. Only in the burgeoning cult of Rían-àr can the people find succour.

# Where's Papa?

I suppose, if we were honest, by the time we reached Papa Westray both Antony and I were already just a little bit weirded out. It had been a beautiful day, and we'd cycled up the length of the larger Orcadian island of Westray, stopping only to boil up cockles on a perfect white sand beach and visit an archaeological site at the Knowe of Skea. Here affable archaeologists (mind you, have you ever met one who wasn't affable?) gave of their time to tell us about the dig. It was an Iron Age sacred site of some kind, the corpses of 127 people bound and interred in the walls of a series of buildings used for metalworking. 'Basically,' our guide told us, 'these people were metal-bashing while granny rotted in the wainscoting.'

There was no one besides us on the ferry across to Papay, as it's locally known. Antony chatted with our genial Charon, while I observed the bank of sea mist, which, having remained offshore throughout the day, was now oozing in. At Moclett Pier a lady was waiting in her car. She wore a blue tunic and took receipt of a prescription from the ferryman. 'Do you want a lift up to Beltane House?' she asked, but we declined. Fiona was, it transpired, our hostess, as well as the district nurse. 'And will chicken be all right for supper, because he's got it on?' Chicken, we conceded, would be fine.

We traversed a dwarfish golf course with only one hole and crossed by the shore of the Loch of St Tredwell. This was the uttermost end of Orkney, with nothing due north of it save for Fair Isle, where men are men and jumpers are nervous. Papay is a diminutive island, four miles long and barely a mile wide in places, but it supports a big history. St Tredwell, the remains of whose chapel stand beside the loch, was one of the 'holy virgins' who accompanied St Boniface on his mission to convert the Picts. Apparently, when some venal fellow saw fit to compliment the nascent saint on her fine eyes, she responded by tearing them out and sending them to him stuck on a bodkin. How's that for anti-vanity!

225

There's Tredwell and there's the Traills, who for centuries were the lairds of Papay. Their big pile, which weights down the middle of the island with its austere vernacular chunkiness, is dubbed 'Holland', because of some Traill's dubious notion that this green lozenge resembled the fertile polders of the Netherlands. The Traills were your typical vile, Highland landowners, racking the rents of their tenants and putting them to work on the noisome and foul business of kelp-making. The Traills are long since gone, but their legacy remains all over the island in the form of abandoned crofts, many of them falling to pieces. Of course, Antony can't see an abandoned croft without wanting to re-tenant it.

So, Antony rummaged around in a tumbledown cabin, while I sat and smoked. He emerged with some lurid recipe books from the 1950s, featuring Day-Glo illustrations of vegetarian cutlets. Oh, and there was also a needlework guide. Finally we reached Beltane House, a B&B-cum-hostel run by the island co-op, to find that 'he', our culinary nemesis, was waiting with the chicken. Lots of chicken and lots of gravy – boat after boat of it sailed to our table and slathered itself over croft-sized mounds of potatoes and chapels of roast fowl. After a wedge of gateau leaking refined sugar, we called for mercy and set out to burn some of the calories off.

The sea mist had rolled right in by now, and the windsock at the dinky little airport (the shortest scheduled flight in the world is from Westray to Papa Westray: two minutes), hung limp in the gloaming. Apart from 'Him' and 'Her' at Beltane House we'd met no one on the island. We wandered through the farms, past old threshing barns. Even the cattle in the fields looked like isolated figures: all of them cut off from the herd. At this latitude it never really gets dark at night, only eerie. We came upon St Boniface's, an austere little kirk on the seashore, four-square, its churchyard planted thick with carious headstones.

'I've got to admit,' Antony's normally resolute basso dropped to a whisper, 'that this place is starting to get to me.' I peered in through the grimy window and stared at the kirk's interior, then turned to my companion: 'Would it get to you more,' I said levelly, 'if I told you that my dead parents were sitting in one of the pews in there talking to St Tredwell?'

'Yeah, OK,' he conceded, 'that is a seriously disturbing image.'

'Not for St Tredwell,' I laughed maniacally, 'or me for that matter. It's you she wants. I told you not to take that needlework guide from the croft.'

# Sweaty Hearth

'Extreme heat locates the individual within the natal cleft of existence,' says Dr Thurm Angström, who I went to interview this week in his claustrophobic office at Reading University's Department of Comparative Environmental Science. Dr Angström's weighty tome, *Sweaty Hearth: Transliterating Domestic Space in the Age of Climate Change*, has been the surprise, beach-book hit of this summer. Apparently it's being lapped up all the way from Ibiza to Mykonos and back again, although the reflective, gold-foiled cover has a tendency to slide from between well-lubricated fingers.

Dr Angström isn't altogether surprised by his populist success, although a recent appearance on the Richard & Judy Book Club left him reeling: 'I couldn't understand why they insisted on larding me with make-up and then sitting me under intense studio lighting. It would've been so much more fitting to have interviewed me in the open air.' Indeed, for open air is what Dr Angström's thesis is all about: 'In the future we will make love and defecate in the garden, while reserving our social life for airily appointed salons . . .' is the arresting opening to his book.

'I'm not an apostle for this wholesale change in our use of domestic space. I am only describing the inevitable,' Dr Angström told me, although on meeting him in person I found this difficult to believe; for the 'Hot Doc' – as he is known in academic circles – was entirely nude save for an Amerindian penis sheath, while a flocculent mass of beard squatted on his muscular chest, suggesting that he was continually nuzzling a small, brown bear. 'We will find ourselves in the next half-century,' he continued, while sponging down his equally flocculent armpits, 'quite casually abandoning our overheated interiors in pursuit of an al fresco home life that will utterly transform our social relations. The garden, the allotment, the patio, the terrace, these will be our new living spaces; while in our houses we will engage in the sacred rituals of computer banking and on-line shopping.'

'But what about people who live in flats?' I objected. 'Surely this brave new world will not be for them.'

'Aha!' The Hot Doc leapt up and began rooting in a filing cabinet. 'That's just where you're wrong.' He thrust an artist's impression into my sweaty hands. It depicted Heath Robinson contraptions, cantilevered decks that extended from the façades of multi-storey blocks. On them men, women and even children cavorted, all of them wearing penis sheaths remarkably like Angström's own. 'Why are the women wearing penis sheaths?' I objected, but he waved me away: 'A mere detail!'

'What about the children?' I objected. 'Surely they'll plummet off these decks?'

'But that's just it!' He began trying to pace up and down, although given the restricted floor area all he could manage was a side-to-side rocking motion, reminiscent of a caged animal. 'In the future up, down, sideways – these will be but contingent facts; the only absolute will be space itself. Our children will be like the Navajo who have no fear of heights whatsoever; freed from the tyranny of interiority they will scamper about the city like the great apes they so manifestly are!'

'Look,' he continued, offering me a half-full bottle of warm Evian, 'already the summer months are seeing you once-uptight Britishers bare as never before! You hang out in your Day-Glo cycling shorts, barbecuing fatty sausages and giving it – how you say – large. You oil yourselves then cavort in paddling pools – which are really only outside baths; can't you see that you're on the verge of a new age of primitivism and abandonment? Soon they will be selling timeshares in Swindon, I tell you . . .'

I can't deny that I was impressed by Dr Angström's passion; yet before I boarded my waiting rickshaw and set off for Reading Station, I felt it incumbent on me to speak with one of his colleagues, Dr Maria Vargas Llama, and discover what this equally eminent environmental scientist thought about the author of *Sweaty Hearth*. 'The man is completely off his chump,' said Dr Llama, extracting a Cohiba Robusto from his gleaming silver humidor and lighting it with a spar of rare hardwood. 'This has nothing to do with global warming – and everything to do with Angström's office.'

'When we moved to this new building,' Dr Llama continued, sitting down behind his huge desk, squarely in the jet of icy air from his massive air-con unit, 'Thurm got the short straw in the office lottery. Up until then he'd specialised in Inuit ice-building techniques. His doctoral thesis was entitled "Frigid Duvet". You gullible journalists,' he airily waved his stogie, 'should dig a little deeper before you splash contentious environmental theories across the newspapers. Most of them aren't about the warming world at all – only this or that stuffy, academic department.'

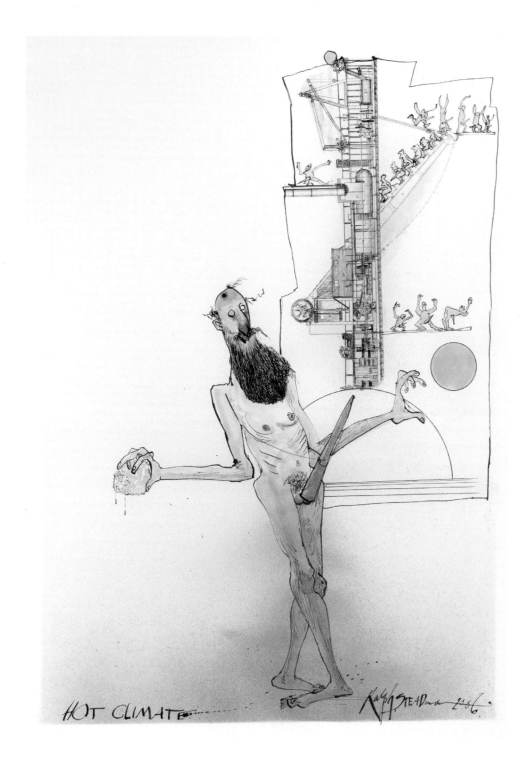

HOT CLIMATE

# Pink, Fluffy Barcelona

Everyone loves Gaudí, no? The last time I was in Barcelona, having four hours to kill between work engagements and no knowledge of the city at all, I asked my hostess to take me to the cathedral. In fairness to her she was only doing the right and literal thing when she took me to La Catedral de la Seu, the city's Gothic pile. But of course I meant Gaudí's masterpiece, La Sagrada Família, the melting-candle towers of which I could see over the urban hugger-mugger, once I ascended to the rooftop in a moderately priced lift.

This time there were to be no such confusions. No sooner had my thirteen-year-old daughter and I checked into our hotel on Avenue Paral-lel than we dived back into the metro. Together with whole legions of other teenage girls we converged on those phallic spires, our hearts full of joy, our squeaky voices still squeakier with enthusiasm – as if we had inhaled helium mixed with laughing gas.

Because everyone loves Gaudí: no other architect has impressed his vision as vitally on a major city as the Catalonian trickster has on Barcelona. Is it too weird to suppose that he knew what he was up to with his sinuous curves, his natural fractals, his hallucinogenic mushrooms, his flower petals and his lingams? That even a century ago Gaudí could descry the future and saw a dark blue sky, close to the end of history, across which snaked the spermy contrails of a myriad low-cost airlines? Planes that would bring to his beloved city a vast – and yet representative – sample of young, global womanhood?

For what is contemporary Barcelona, in the holiday season, save a gigantic urban sorority? So feminising is the tendency of Gaudí's sinuous curves that they gather into themselves an thousand, thousand orthodontically challenged, navel-pierced, Justin Timberlake fans, all of them gum-chewing, twittering, preening and prancing to the tinny beat of their iPods. I felt this great tide of femininity at the very core of my being, and found myself almost surfing on its current of hormones, felt

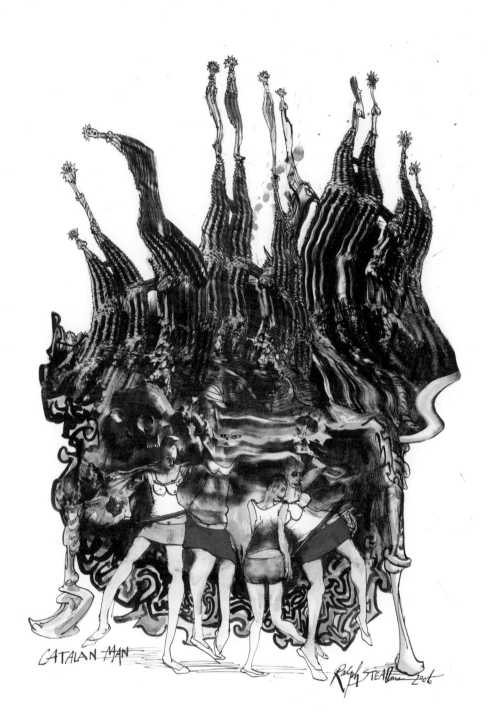

CATALAN MAN

Ralph STEADman 2006

my breasts swell and my lingam shrivel to the dimensions of a mere architectural detail.

But back to the unfinished cathedral: everyone loves Gaudí, no? Loves the idea that La Sagrada Família is the truest of modern Gothic, in its praxis if not its form. For, unlike contemporary, flat-pack edifices, this staggering stalagmite of a building has been dripped into existence over decades, a slow accretion handed down from Gaudí daddy to Gaudí son in much the same way that the great medieval cathedrals were built. Inside its tracery of gushing buttresses – which spurt skywards in a dense cage of scaffolding – you feel this praxis intently, a highly sexual stridulation of steel rubbing against stone.

Yes, everyone loves Gaudí, except that close up La Sagrada Família is just a little bit . . . Well, what is the mot juste . . . ? Just a little bit ugly. That's it. Because the holy figures on the façade have the Cubist features not of angelic beings but of that crude puppet once used to advertise Cuprinol wood preservative (a puppet which, bizarrely, was kidnapped and held to ransom, but that's another story). And the flying buttresses that stretch from this façade into the forecourt: well, perhaps it's the presence of entire herds of heifers chewing their latex cud, but they are rather reminiscent of Wrigley twists between girlish teeth. And the finials, spires and pinnacles of the sacred edifice (a building likened by a contemporary of Gaudí's to a 'pile of chicken giblets'): while their bright colours and fruity form, and their incorporation of traditional Catalan mosaic, give them a certain trippy quality, this is not the artificial paradise of a Baudelaire or a Coleridge, but an altogether more cuddly noumenal realm.

Don't get me wrong: everyone loves Gaudí – and I'm no exception. La Sagrada Família wins me over with its sheer wantonness as a building – this is the Lolita of sacred architecture. But it isn't until a couple of days later, when we venture further north to the Parc Güell, Gaudí's botched attempt at building a garden suburb, that the conundrum of his unique vision is finally resolved for me. Yes, it is modernist, yes, he took Art Nouveau and gave it several more twists into the mystical, yet observing the dinky gatehouses of the park, their pie-crust roofs and organic windows, I was reminded, not of anything remotely sublime, but of the kitsch dwellings of those animated Belgian munchkins, the Smurfs. I half expected Father Abraham to emerge from behind one, monstrously large and speaking baby-Walloon.

It is this infantilism that explains why everyone loves Gaudí, I think. This desire we all have to be a pink, fluffy girl in her pink, fluffy bedroom. And in our kidult era, what could be more loveable than a kidult genius of the built environment?

# The Art of Lobster

On the expansive balcony of the Hotel Arts, overlooking the Barcelona port area, I listen to the following conversation: 'Today, sir, can I recommend the seared tuna steak, which is very excellent?'

'Look, I gotta tellya right off: I'm from, like, North Carolina, and if there's one thing we have there it's the best goddamn tuna in the world; so, I'm, like, tuna sore, if you know what I mean.'

'Certainly, sir, I quite understand.' The waiter is impeccably neutral. He looks Belgian – all the staff here appear Low Country. They wear understated uniforms, baggy khaki trousers, striped linen shirts. They also all look as if they have degrees in art history, which is no surprise given that the whole shtick of this luxury hotel is its collection of fine art works.

'Do these lobsters come from, like, Maine? Coz 150 euros is a helluva lot to pay for a lobster.' It's only because I'm actually reading a sensitive, humane, funny and fiercely intelligent novel by an American friend while I listen to this clod – with his 'Buttons Hawaii' baseball cap and his black and maroon 'rising sun' motif shorts, and his nonce connectives – that I don't, like, collapse into rabid, internal anti-Americanism. There's this, and the fact that I myself hold a US passport.

'I'm not sure, sir, I will check with chef and see what he says.' The doctoral servitor pads away. O! The Hotel Arts, with your sun-drenched terraces and your rooftop garden full of palms; with your whispering, air-conditioned corridors and your elegant lobbies crammed with the toned and upholstered bodies of the rich! Why is it that I feel about as relaxed in such environs as a scrotum with a razorblade poised beneath it? Luxury – I just don't sit well with it. Comfort I can broker, but luxury is non-negotiable. It's the way that I can't open the picture window in my room that really alienates me. This sets up a fundamental antinomy between hotel/not hotel, that renders the whole experience nauseating. The Hotel Arts could be

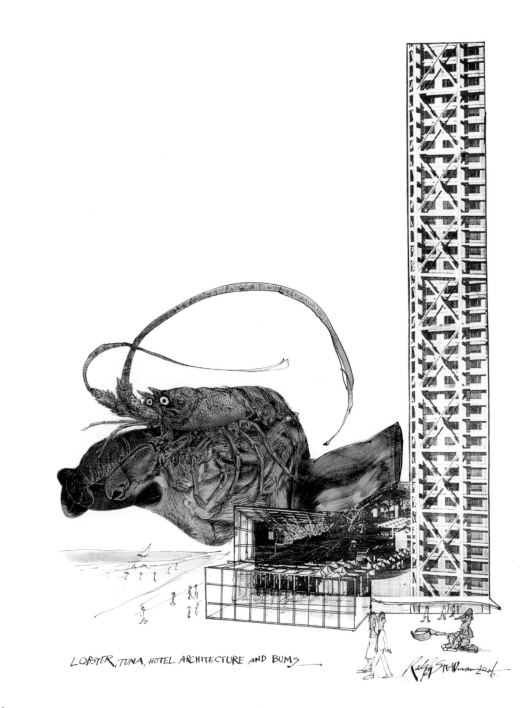

LOBSTER, TUNA, HOTEL ARCHITECTURE AND BUMS

Ralph Steadman 2006

anywhere – orbiting Uranus even. It certainly isn't in Spain, with its international staff and nouveau-riche clientele.

It probably doesn't help that I feel compelled to watch rolling news on plasma screen TV in my room. The juxtaposition between the pulverised villages of southern Lebanon and the brushed aluminium, smoked glass and leatherette fittings is grotesque in the extreme. I decide to film the whole scene with my digital camera in the hope that by doubly distancing myself I will somehow dock with the hotel and thus enter a secure orbit around my own hypocrisy. No dice. As I pan and zoom into the bathroom – which is the size of a Hezbollah bunker – I catch sight of my mad, Anthony Perkins rictus in the full-length mirror. Damn it! If things continue like this, I'll stab myself in the shower.

It didn't help that on the way here, while changing trains at the Plaça de Catalunya, I was looped in by a peculiarly efficient beggar. He performed that unearthly trick street people have of projecting his voice into my inner ear as I paced along the platform, chatting to my daughter: 'It's great to hear an English voice,' he said in a rusty Mancunian accent; and had me in that moment, for I stopped, turned and engaged with him. Whereas, had he encountered me straight on, I would've been on guard against his sweaty baseball cap and moribund khaki shorts.

He set out his spiel with a stallholder's efficiency as I stared into his eager, bloodshot eyes: there was a baggage handlers' strike at the airport – we better watch out! He had to get back to work, so his brother had bought him a Ryanair ticket out of Madrid. There was only one problem – and this came after some minutes of chit-chat, so I was completely gulled – he needed another 10 euros to get there. I gave him twenty without demurral: in my experience commerce renders public space domesticated, so we were huddled together in his front parlour, rather than forming a small, Anglo-Saxon baffler, around which the Hispanic multitude flowed.

'I'm not a bum!' he protested, taking the note. 'Give me your email address and I'll make sure you get it back!' But he most certainly was a bum – and I never would, and besides I was already striding away, daughter in tow. 'I'm not a bum!' His cry came back to me now as I sat, sipping my tonic water and munching my cob salad complete with half the dratted lobster. The waiter closed in again on the bum from North Carolina at the next table: 'They're from Maine, sir,' he said.

'Wossat?' The bum looked up from romancing his girlfriend, who wore Dolce & Gabbana sunglasses and pearly-pink lip gloss.

'The lobsters, sir, they are from Maine.'

' – and undoubtedly off,' I put my oar in, 'given that there's a baggage handlers' strike at the airport . . .'

# I Am a Cable Car

Through the warp and weft of memory – thick threads of confabulation, thin filaments of recollection – we are back in Barcelona. My daughter Madeleine and I, walking down through the Jardins de Miramar, the city spread out beneath us, a curiously homely collection of blocks and spires. I'm a little wobbly on my pins, overcome by the adrenalin rush of having survived a terrifying ordeal: the cable car ride across the harbour.

I'd spotted the cable car a couple of days before, when we stepped out of our hotel on Paral-lel. Spotted the curved line the cable drew across the azure sky, spotted the winking jewel of the car, and blurted out, 'Ooh, look, there's a cable car', while my internal voice screamed, 'Don't mention it! She'll want to go on it right away!' And, of course, she did, because Maddie is thirteen and has absolutely no fear of heights, whereas I am forty-four and suffer tachycardia if I have to fetch a suitcase down from the attic.

I held off for a couple of days, whining all the time, while she expertly coaxed me towards our doom, saying: 'We don't have to go if you don't want to.' Bringing up father, eh, isn't that way it's always been? So, we walked along the front at Barceloneta, past families cavorting on the packed sand, past a lurid, cartoon poster of a man in fish-scale swimming trunks wrestling with a giant cigarette butt; all the while the debate continued and the wind whipped in off the sea.

Up ahead lowered the Torre de St Sebastià, a horrible, workaday Martian tripod, poised on the dockside and tethered by the cable to its master, the Torre Jaume 1. I could see the ludicrous little death box inching between them, dangling over the municipal void. I could imagine its bucking motion. I felt as I always feel when about to embark on these mundane and fearful transports: I am a prosaic character in a Dostoevsky novel, edited out of an early draft. I cast my maddened eye about me at the world I am about to leave behind, and swear to myself that, should I survive the ordeal, I will never again take for granted this fresh breeze, this sparkling sunlight, that Volvo showroom.

At the base of the tower, where you buy your tickets before entering the lift, someone had added a graffito to the sign portraying the cable car, so that it appeared to be depended from an enormous, hypodermic syringe. My heart shifted up another gear. But if it was windy at sea level, 300 feet up on the open platform Aeolus was playing frantic bebop. I became cringingly garrulous in order to combat my anxiety. I chatted up two elderly American women; a genial, bald Italian with a camcorder; a Scandinavian honeymoon couple. But it was no good: I was still absolutely certain that as soon as I climbed aboard the cable car (which I could now see was absurdly tiny, a phone box in space), I would vomit and faint simultaneously.

Luckily the camera came to the rescue. I'd been snapping stills the whole way along the promenade; now, as the cable car lurched away from the tower, I began shooting full-motion. It worked: as I was looking at a tiny little image of the drop, obviously I couldn't possibly be above it. That wasn't a real waiter setting up a table on the upper deck of that concrete cruise liner, the Barcelonan World Trade Center – but a Hollywood extra. Maddie's hair flared around her face as she craned through the open windows of the car, but I felt no neurotic terror, I simply panned about me, a Stanley Kubrick of a tourist, shooting a Vietnam war movie in Docklands.

When the cable car finally reached the Plaça de l'Armada and we clambered out, I felt as fluttery as an angel. I had survived! I was a changed man. I would be kind to all from henceforth! As we trudged back down to the city we entered another circle of hell. In among the scrubby trees were discarded syringes, DIY crack pipes, a human turd poised on a sheet of cardboard. Scattered about were official-looking papers. I stopped, picked them up. They were the graduation certificates of a certain Massimiliano X from the Accademia di Belle Arti in Rome. Massimiliano had been studying scenografia and regia, then had come to Barcelona for an extension course – this much the papers told me. But had he made the crack pipe and set fire to his nascent career? Or had some junky stolen his bag, then scattered the papers?

I resolved to take them home to London with me. There was an address in Pedara, I would write to Massimiliano and find out his story. I owed it to him, as one film director to another.

# Wild Water

The river: it enfolds us in its icy embrace. Superficially, it isn't turbid, only an insistent, coiled, supremely powerful inertia. Stop swimming for an instant, and I can feel it push me downstream at a steady 2 mph. There are seven of us abreast, holding to the centre of the Avon; the river is chilly with the run-off of the August rainstorms, and our engagement with the water is profound and elemental. The Avon takes us all and subsumes us to its own relentless pulsion. The heads of my fellow swimmers are otter-sleek as they dip and rise. We are no longer human, I feel, as we contemplate the grassy banks, only understudies for some yet-to-be-realised production of *The Wind in the Willows*.

Charles – whose land runs along the bank – chooses this moment, with supreme tact, to tell us about the 450-lb pike he's recently seen stuffed in a local museum. A pike caught in this very river. At once our white legs and whiter bellies are lures flickering beneath the surface; the ancient, bony fish are rising from the river bed, intent on teaching us a lesson, sending us back to our tiled paddling pools with a vengeance. We do not belong here – we belong there, minus a limb. Or two.

It's been a summer of wild-water swimming for me. As middle age advances I feel myself more and more drawn to plunging into lakes, tarns, rivers and, of course, the sea. The wild-water swimmers' guru was the writer and broadcaster Roger Deakin, who very sadly died last month, aged only sixty-three. His book *Waterlog* told the story of his peculiar, liquid odyssey across Britain, splashing off the Scillies, plashing on Dartmoor, breasting the chalk-bed stream of the Itchen, tumbling down watery chutes in the Yorkshire Dales. It's a beautiful, melancholic and yet intensely celebratory account of one man's total immersion in our environment and I urge you all to read it.

Deakin wasn't just a wild-water swimming enthusiast – he was a campaigner for the rights of us all to roam as freely in liquid as we would like to on land. Agencies,

councils, fishing clubs and landowners are all intent on barring the swimmer from the swim. They scaremonger with Weil's disease, a nasty rat-borne malaise which can be avoided with simple precautions, such as not swimming with open wounds on your body. However, the risks of 'rough' swimming are obvious: fish hooks, currents, whirlpools, cramps, pike and weed – a gamut of challenges which healthily affirm that you are where you ought to be: in the welter of the world, not a place apart.

I've swum this year in the Avon, the Thames, Loch Lomond; and in the sea, off the Orcadian island of Westray, Hurst Beach in the Solent, Barcelona, Ibiza, and many times at Brighton. The practice never jades me, each fresh dousing only invigorates. The land seen from wild water is another country, waiting to be rediscovered as you stagger ashore, while the water itself cradles you in its diluvian embrace.

I so loved my wild-water swimming this summer that I couldn't bear the season to end. I dragged the kids down to Brighton for a final float in choppy waves, staring up at the rococo madness of the Palace Pier. Back, banged up in London's prison, I found myself last weekend on Hampstead Heath, and went to swim in Highgate men's pond.

It was a long time since I'd swum there, and I noted that the chest-waxers – who for years have been in the ascendant – have now all but eased out that other moiety: nude, pot-bellied, old Jewish men playing hard ball. No matter – and no matter either that the pond, fed from the source of the River Fleet, probably isn't natural at all, but an exercise in Georgian landscaping. The important thing is that its margins are muddy, it's surrounded by trees and grass, and the peerlessly elegant forms of swans glide across it. Still, the stentorian notice warning of the presence of blue-green algae in the water was off-putting.

I ignored it and dove right in. After all, I'd ignored the signs that said you shouldn't swim off Hurst Beach, and I'd shamelessly swum outside the coastguard flags on Brighton Beach. I'd even ignored the plague of jellyfish infesting the Mediterranean. But for how long can this go on? Deakin's book took its inspiration from a John Cheever story 'The Swimmer', the protagonist of which 'swims home' across the pools and rivers of his New England district. We all want to swim home, don't we, and dive into that natal cleft? Yet I fear we're all about to be landed, gutted, stuffed, and put on display in a local museum.

# Beard in Space

I love Richard Branson. I love his beautiful beard and his twinkly blue eyes. I love his homely knighthood and his adventurous manhood. I love his vision and his sheer, entrepreneurial drive. I simply won't hear a word against him. I think – if he only knew me – that Sir Richard might just love me a little, too; granted I haven't got the kind of body he requires to promote his condoms, or his vodka, or his mobile phones; nor, perhaps, the kind of body he himself would most like to cleave to. And to be absolutely frank: I'm not a virgin. Nevertheless, there's a spark between us, of that much I'm sure; a spark that could ignite a conflagration.

That's why I'm signing up right away for the *Virgin Galactic* spaceship, whose mission is to commercially go where only governments have heretofore been. At £107,000 a ticket, the spaceship represents excellent value for money (a tautology that Sir Ricky and I both understand only too well). After three days' training I will be ushered on board the spaceship, which in turn will be housed on the belly of an aircraft with the virginally romantic name, *White Knight*.

Then it's chocks away, and off we'll go on our two-and-a-half-hour flight. First up to nine miles above the earth's surface; then the spaceship will be released, the clean, green jets will be ignited, and we'll blast at speeds up to 3,000 mph, ninety miles high! Up there we'll see the very curvature of the Earth and the fragility of the precious atmospheric envelope that encloses it. Then the pilot will switch off the 'fasten seatbelts' sign, and for six whole minutes us passengers will float free in the pressurised cabin. Free to sport and tumble, free to appreciate the marvel of our celestial state.

I've no doubt that it's a moving experience, and one that has never failed to transform those who have had it. Up until now, the only people who've been on space flights are dry, unimaginative types: air force pilots, scientists and the like. With the best will in the world, these inarticulate souls have found it next to

impossible to convey to us what it's like to touch the smooth-shaven face of God. But with Ricky-Baby's *Virgin Galactic*, hundreds of dot.com wizards, industrialists, property developers and derivative traders will come face-to-face with the infinite!

Ricardo-the-Brick has said: 'To be able to extend that privilege to people from all walks of life has been a long-held ambition of Virgin.' And who but a churl could doubt that he means it? As is the way with these things, once the service is up and running, and competitors have entered the field (EasyMoon, RyanOrbit), doubtless the prices will come down. Then school dinner ladies, road sweepers, call centre operatives and people on sickness benefit will all cheaply and easily attain this zenith of human travelling possibility.

What a change we'll wreak on our society – and I'm not just talking increased environmental consciousness here. No, this could very well be the dawning of the Third Age prophesied by many sages and futurologists. Doubtless Ricky-Darling will lead the way, by casting off all his worldly ties and chattels, donning a simple (and virginal) white robe, and embarking on a lifestyle characterised by poverty, charity and continence. He will forego his holidays in the Caribbean, making his new slogan: 'Give Mustique back to the Musketeers!' (Or whatever it is the natives are called.) He will stop trying to pretend he can run a rail company, and gift his Pendolinos to the state! He will fill his condoms with his vodka and his cola, and throw them to the baying, saturnalian mob!

Lest we – or rather, I – get carried away with this vision, I must mention one small misgiving: passengers on the *Virgin Galactic* will be expected to waive the company's responsibility for their safety. That's right: if it all goes tits-up (ooh-er! Saucy, eh, Dicky), Our Saviour will have nothing to answer for. But let us not view this as a significant drawback. I'm reliably informed that financiers are already looking into the provision of special, two-and-a-half-hour life insurance policies. Isn't that amazing? Truly, Brandy (as I understand he's known to his bosom buddies) is a veritable inspirer of innovation in all fields.

What next? Perhaps we'll be able to insure ourselves against trains being late, or condoms splitting, or vodka making us lose our jobs and beat up our partners? The possibilities, surely, are endless. And it's in this spirit that we shouldn't allow mere considerations of personal safety to stop us from picking up that phone and making that booking. No need to worry if you haven't got the £107,000 to pay cash down, Dickhead is 'democratising' space travel, so a mere two million air miles clocked up on his mundane aircraft will also secure you a ticket. Huzzah!

# Romantic Services

At Tebay Services, between junctions 38 and 39 on the M6, a brass ensemble parps and poots its way through a selection of festive ditties. Up here, in the north, there is a notable shift in the appearance of the generality of mankind, and the Dr David Kelly/Dr Harold Shipman phenotype predominates. Many, many men, lost in the fastness of late middle age, their grey beards spade-shaped, their cardigans tightly buttoned, the lenses of their sensible glasses reflecting the phenomenal offers available: £14.99 for a black-and-white, fourteen-inch television, complete with cigarette lighter plug adaptor. Oh, to buy one! Then drive the rest of the way to Scotland with one eye on the humped whale-back of the motorway, and the other on *Saturday Night and Sunday Morning*. Albert Finney in a string vest, Rachel Roberts in her slip. Bliss.

Instead, I munch a cheese selection – Boursin, smoked German, Wensleydale – and look out over the ornamental duck pond, to where the Cumbrian Fells loom and lower. Tebay is easily the best motorway services in the British Isles. It has an authentic country kitchen and a farm shop (opened by the heir to the throne in 2004). It is also a family-run business, staffed by local people, and instead of the bland featurelessness of most service centres, Tebay, with its rough-textured stone buildings, seems to pre-date the M6, rather than being a mere outgrowth of the motorway.

Indeed, as the tubas honk and the ducks bib and bob, I find myself transported back to an earlier, more romantic era. Perhaps the poet Samuel Taylor Coleridge, on one of his legendary stomps across the Lake District, chanced upon Tebay Services, all huddled beneath its high gables. I like to imagine the great idealist, sweating off an opium binge in the Westmorland Hotel, while bemoaning his failure to win the heart of fair 'Asra'. Meanwhile, Sara Hutchinson, that sturdy lass, is being tupped senseless by William Wordsworth in the next bedroom. Later,

POET'S CORNER

Wordsworth will retrieve his fustian breeches from the trouser press, and with his legendary fastidiousness make them both a cup of tea, adding one small container of UHT milk to hers.

If only I could stay here in Tebay for all of 2007. But why stop at a single year? If I reside at Tebay for long enough, the M6 will fall into desuetude and become grassed over, a second pre-industrial age will dawn and, instead of glib satires, lyrical ballads will flow from my pen. No dice: 'That willing suspension of disbelief for the moment, which constitutes poetic faith' is gone. Instead, I load up the family, ejaculate forty odd litres of low-sulphur unleaded into the black womb of the Fiat, and head north.

What a strange interregnum the Christmas season is: the British people forsake their gainful employment and take to the roads for a fortnight, en masse, forming an atomised caravan of Hyundais, Volvos and Chevrolet Voyagers. In a peculiar inversion of the ways of our forbears, we made the round of visits, relatives and friends, but rather than a gentle progress of a couple of score miles, we drove for hundreds, the length and breadth of the country. In Jane Austen novels, if the Misses Bennett got a slight cold, they would impose on their hosts for weeks. By contrast, we stop to see the relatives for a few hours then motor all day to stock up on Vick's nasal spray at the next services.

I calculate that between 23 December and 2 January I did a full thirty-five-hour week behind the wheel. I drove so far that I visited both the northbound and the southbound Southwaite Services (between junctions 42 and 41 on the M6) twice. Suitably enough, the season ended in Tinshell Services between junctions 29 and 28 on the southbound carriageway of the M1. This is an ancient, industrial landscape: the Drax Power Station cooling towers rising up over the flatlands like malevolent, smoking deities. Tinshell is a cold comfort car farm. There's no brass band – there are no rustic gables. In the Wimpy where I buy the kiddies their junk food fix, the staff display their occupational stigmata: dreadful acne.

The time since the men's toilets were last cleaned is inscribed by red, LED letters: 'Aeons'. We have been weighed in the balance and found wanting; that's why Tinshell is so chilly, so dreadfully mundane. The kids want to disappear into a booth advertised as 'Van Gogh's Colour Studio' – but I fear for their little ears and so I palm them off with 20p's worth of jelly beans. Does it have to end like this? The Dr David Kelly phenotypes moribund in this unbeauty spot? I crack, and we spend the next three hours on the motorway watching Laurence Olivier and Greer Garson. It is a truth universally acknowledged, that a man in possession of £14.99 must be in want of a car television.

# Newfoundland

Thanks, Mum. Were it not for your obsessive diary-keeping I might never have known that I once traversed the Atlantic by ship. True, I did have a jellyfish of a memory, a two-year-old's gelatinous perceptions, trawled from deep time, and refracted by the waters of Lethe: a much-loved teddy bear with corduroy ears, round portholes, a white-painted railing . . . Er, that's it. But your diary really does the business, Mum, setting down our 1963 crossing from Southampton to Quebec in all its prosaic detail.

How I sympathise with my father, who on the night preceding departure is introduced thus: 'A tired Peter packed last night – reluctant but he did it.' I, too, have the greatest difficulty in packing, and sometimes think I would travel more if there were an identical set of my own effects at every prospective destination. Presumably that's what the very rich – and fascist dictators – aspire to.

On board the *Franconia*, as the ship beat down the Channel, my mother set down in her diary a combination of geographical ignorance and rather touching arrogance: 'Today we are off the coast of Cornwall: I thought it was Ireland, but another lady thought it was Scotland, so I've at least not exceeded her.' Meanwhile, my older brother and I were soon behaving uncannily like my own small boys: 'W threw 2 pieces of potato on the floor, J dipped his head and got a spoonful of minced chicken in his eye.'

As on any sea voyage, mealtimes seem to have been the chief focus for social interaction, and Mum's inevitable disapprobation: 'Two young American girls at our table last night, going back to Calif. after a year in France. I took an instant dislike to them, for their smug expectation that the glories of France were for them. Was I ever so lacking in humbleness?' Mum was American herself, but while her countrywomen's sense of entitlement bothered her, the Atlantic terrified her: 'In the night I awoke to clothing swaying on hooks & Willie.' (That's me.) 'I sat on

the easy chair with him & felt so happy & lucky. This morning both of them were ill, so we dressed them and took them on deck for fresh air. A very long day. I saw the imminent breaking up of the ship every moment, & ourselves & our beautiful young drowning in hideously cold & salty water.'

Not to be facetious, but would a freshwater inundation have been any better? Poor Mum: not only subject to this marine neurosis, but also to my father's watery analysis: 'V. tired,' she writes two days later, 'Peter rightly says it's my "disposition" – anxiety tires one. I am quite exhausted.' Still, when not worn out by small children and the vast ocean, Mum did find time to cast a jaundiced eye over herself and her husband: 'I look very lumpy & unattractive in my clothes, my face looks worn. P has developed a great lump of varicose veins on his leg. I can't think my looks are all age – but some, perhaps.' She was, of course, five years younger than I am now.

However, the most pleasing entry in the diary comes when the *Franconia* draws near to North America: 'Sun & wind today, steely gray waves, long line of land on the horizon (Newfoundland) & a rocky looking mountain (Belle Isle?). P said he met someone who had been shipwrecked here (in 1910?) & had to live weeks on berries.' The whole anecdote is my father to a T – or a P – especially the detail of 'on berries'; I can just hear my father pronouncing this with considerable relish, as if being marooned were an opportunity to re-enact the healthful regimen of an interwar, Fabian summer school.

Other aspects of the diary are not quite so cosy. My parents' marriage was never a tranquil one, and Mum confined every rebarbative misgiving between narrow feint bars. 'These,' she writes at one point, 'are the wages of meaningless marriage.' Which leads me to consider whether or not the virtues of air travel are not emotional quite as much as economic. True, couples can argue quite as well on planes as they once did on liners, yet there isn't the time for this kind of festering despair.

Still, it was all drawing to an end. On 3 September Mum reports: 'Land outside the porthole'; and then, for the next ten days, the *Franconia* wends its way up the St Lawrence 'taking on one pilot after another'. We finally docked in Quebec on the 13th, and the passengers were confined to the non-air-conditioned theatre, while the luggage was offloaded. Here I disgraced myself with diarrhoea, soiling my clothes, and a chair in first class, much to Mum's distraction. Ah! Even at two, I was an anarchist abroad.